Mix & Match

IDEAS for PRE-SCHOOL MINISTRY

Group

Loveland, Colorado

Mix and Match Ideas for Preschool Ministry

CREDITS
Editor: Jan Kershner
Senior Editor: Paul Woods
Chief Creative Officer: Joani Schultz
Copy Editor: Julie Meiklejohn
Designer and Art Director: Jean Bruns
Cover Art Director: Helen H. Lannis
Computer Graphic Artist: Randy Kady
Cover Designer: Diana Walters
Illustrator: Lynn Sweat
Production Manager: Ann Marie Gordon

Unless otherwise noted, Scriptures quoted from The Youth Bible, New Century Version, copyright © 1991 by Word Publishing, Dallas, Texas 75039. Used by permission.

Library of Congress Cataloging-in-Publication Data

Mix and match ideas for preschool ministry / [Jan Kershner, editor].
     p.   cm.
    Ideas taken from Children's ministry magazine.
    Includes index.
    ISBN 0-7644-2021-6
    1. Christian education of preschool children. 2. Christian education—Activity programs.   I. Kershner, Jan.
BV1475.7.M58 1997
268' .432—dc21   97-1963
                                                          CIP

10 9 8 7 6 5 4 3 2   06 05 04 03 02 01 00 99 98 97
Printed in the United States of America.

Contents

Contributing Authors

Our thanks go out to the following authors
for making this book possible.

Susan Anderson
Les Auchmoody
Barbie Ballou
Glenn Bannerman
Jill Barney
Linda Becken
Carol Benoit
Carolyn Beyer
Bobbie Bower
Herbert Brokering
Valerie Brooks
Chris Brown
May Jane Bruce
Mary Casey
Jane McBride Choate
Debbie Clark
Terri Cocanougher
Ada Cooper
Gay Correll
Jean Cozby
Mary Davis
Marcia Flynn
Linda Gilden
Sheila Halasz
Donald Hinchey
Margaret Hinchey
Connie Holman
Kerry Lynn Isett
Ellen Javernick
Christine Johnson
Selma Johnson

Cindy Jones
Nancy Kaczrowski
Carmen Kamrath
Darla Karnes
Becky Knoll
Robyn Kundert
Linda Larson
Charlotte Lesko
Paul Lessard
Morey Levenson
Paula Jo Logan
Cynthia Long
Kayla Major
Deborah Mann
Janet Mason
Carole Meltzer
Dwight Mix
Ruth Mooney
Amy Nappa
Mike Nappa
Sheryl Neely
Cindy Nelson
Debbie Neufeld
Cindy Newell
Beth Newland
Lori Haynes Niles
Walter Norvell
Debbie Trafton O'Neal
Susan Osborn
JoAnn Otto
Anna Page
Leticia Parks

Stephen Parolini
Nancy Paulson
Susan Petty
Lois Putnam
Deborah Fenter Reedy
Carol McAdoo Rehme
Jolene Roehlkepartain
Tammy Ross
Tatta Roth
Deanna Salter
Sarah Searcey
Lisa Seeders
Vicki Shannon
Kathleen Sherbon
Charles Smith
Cindy Smith
Esther Stockwell
Lisa Stone
Susan Stoner
Marcy Tawney
Jim Thomson
Sue Thurston
Jan Tomlinson
Mitch Townley
Greta Van Hemert
Joclyn Wampler
Angela Washburn
Keith Wilson
Evelyn Witter
Christine Yount
Malinda Zellman

Introduction

Need a quick craft for tomorrow's lesson? Stuck for a song for that special program? Wonder how other preschool teachers survive Sunday?

Well, look no further! *Mix and Match Ideas for Preschool Ministry* is a treasure trove of ideas right at your fingertips. And not just any ideas—these are Children's Ministry Magazine's best-ever ideas for preschoolers. Since 1991, Children's Ministry Magazine has been bringing you the most exciting, innovative, teacher-tested ideas on the market.

Now we've taken the best of those ideas—the cream of the crop—and compiled them in this new book. Designed especially for your preschoolers, *Mix and Match Ideas for Preschool Ministry* will become a valuable, versatile tool you'll reach for again and again.

Pick a Bible lesson. Match it with a song and a special seasonal idea. Mix in a game or a craft and voilà—you have an instant lesson. What could be easier? or more fun?

And remember—every idea in this book is teacher-tested and age-appropriate. You'll find complete, ready-to-go Bible lessons, as well as easy story stretchers to enhance existing studies.

You'll also find cooperative games, seasonal activities, singable songs, finger plays, and the best preschool crafts anywhere. And don't forget the terrific helpful-hints section. We've included practical advice from experts all over the country—teachers on the front line, just like you!

So go ahead. Turn the page. Your mix and match adventure is about to begin!

Bible LESSONS & STORY Stretchers

To keep children interested as you tell them Bible truths, try these "do it together" tips:

■Have children act out Bible stories.

■Form teams, and have kids work together to solve a character's problem. For example, have kids decide what Joseph could have done after his brothers deserted him.

■Ask children about their feelings. Ask questions such as "How would you have felt if you were Joseph?" "What would you have done?" or "What did you learn about...?"

■Open a Bible study with a game. For example, chant "Going on a Lion Hunt" (adapted from the chant "Going on a Bear Hunt") before the story of Daniel and the lions' den.

And Bible Story Stretchers can be great tools to spice up your Bible lessons. They're easy, they're quick, and they're flexible. Just replace not-so-exciting activities or add Story Stretchers to your lessons to capture kids' attention.

Use the following Bible lessons to lead your preschoolers in their growing faith. (And never fear—no matter what happens, it probably won't be as bad as the teacher's tale at the end of this chapter!)

BIBLE LESSONS

A New Kind of Fishing

THEME: Jesus can make us fishers of men.
SCRIPTURES: Matthew 4:18-22; Luke 5:1-11; or John 21:1-14

Make a "fishing pond" by placing a circle of blue fabric on the floor. Lay small rocks around the pond. Cut large fish out of construction paper, and attach a paper clip to each fish. Scatter the fish around the pond.

Make a fishing pole for each child by tying one end of a two-foot piece of string to a small magnet and stapling the other end to a yardstick or a 3-foot stick. Give each child a pole to reel in the paper fish.

After all the fish are caught, give each child several small construction paper squares. Help children glue the colorful pieces of paper to their fish to make fish mosaics.

Then read and discuss any of the following stories: Jesus calls his disciples to be fishers of men (Matthew 4:18-22); Peter's great catch of fish (Luke 5:1-11); or Jesus cooks breakfast for the disciples (John 21:1-14).

Kids may want to go fishing again!

Manner Mania

THEME: Love has good manners.
SCRIPTURE: Luke 6:31

Here's a quick primer to develop each of your kids into a little Miss or Mister Manners.

■ **KINDNESS CROWNS**—Draw a crown outline on yellow construction paper for each child. Help children cut out their crowns. Set out star stickers or crayons for children to use to decorate their crowns.

As children are working, say: **These crowns show that you belong to God's kingdom and that you'll try to be kind.**

Help kids staple the ends of their crowns together so they can wear the crowns during class.

■**GOLDEN RULE**—When the crowns are completed, march around the room and have the children follow you as they chant, "We're kids of the King!"

Then have children sit in a circle. Read aloud Luke 6:31. Say: **God wants us to love each other. One way to show love is by using good manners. When we're polite at the table, when we answer the phone nicely, and when we don't interrupt other people as they're talking, we're using good manners. Using good manners means treating other people the way we like to be treated. And this makes God happy!**

■**PARTY MANNERS**—Say: **Let's plan a birthday party so we can practice our manners!** Appoint a host or hostess. Encourage kids to help plan decorations, games, and other birthday party fun. Provide inflated balloons and streamers for kids to use to decorate the room.

Help children use imaginative play to practice good manners in the party setting. Look for these manners: the host or hostess greeting the other children, guests offering a birthday greeting and an imaginary gift, guests saying, "Yes, please" or "No, thank you" when offered cake and ice cream, and guests thanking the host or hostess when the party is over.

Serve cake and ice cream, and encourage kids to use their best manners as they pass plates and eat. Remind kids that one good table manner is not talking with food in their mouths.

After the party is over, praise the children for their good manners. To close, have children hold hands in a circle. Then pray: **Thank you, God, for letting us show our love through good manners. Amen.**

Mission Impossible?

THEME: God can do all things.
SCRIPTURE: Matthew 14:22-33

Use the following activities to help kids believe that God can do the impossible.

■**POSSIBLE OR IMPOSSIBLE?**—Have children tell you about one of their favorite cartoons or movies. When a child mentions something that's possible or impossible for a character to do, ask:

● **Would that be possible for someone to do in real life?**

Why or why not?

Say: **Sometimes it's hard to tell which things on television are really real and which are only pretend. Television can look very real, but not everything on television is true or even possible. The people who make TV shows use tricks to make things look possible when they're really not.**

■**FANTASY BOOK**—Say: **You were good at telling me which things were impossible in the cartoon** (or movie). **Let's see if you can tell which things are impossible in a book.**

Read any short fantasy book such as *The Cat in the Hat* by Dr. Seuss or *Just a Daydream* by Mercer Mayer. Discuss which things in the book couldn't happen in real life and which things could.

■**POSSIBILITY**—Say: **Now I want to tell you a story from the Bible, and I want you to tell me if what happened in the story is possible or impossible.**

Read or paraphrase Matthew 14:22-33, the story of Jesus walking on the water. Ask:

● **Is this story possible or impossible? Explain.**
● **How could Jesus walk on water?**
● **Why can't we walk on water?**
● **Is there anything God can't do? If so, what?**

Say: **The nice thing about anything we read in the Bible is that it's always true and always possible. God can do anything, even if it seems impossible to us. You may not always be sure of everything on television or in books, but you can always be sure of God and the words in the Bible. The Bible is always true. And with God, all things are possible.**

■**WALK ON WATER**—Give each child two plastic-foam meat trays. Tell each child to take his or her shoes and socks off and place one foot over one of the trays. Help children use a sharp pencil to trace around their feet on their meat trays.

Help children cut out their feet outlines. When they're finished, lead children to a sink or large tub of water. Have children take turns floating their plastic-foam feet in the water. Say: **Use these feet in your bathtub or sink at home to retell the story about Jesus walking on the water to your parents.**

■**FLOATS**—Before snack time, pray: **Dear God, thank you for this snack. May we always know that you're the only one who can do the impossible. Amen.**

Serve glasses of lemon-lime soda with sherbet floating on top.

Helpful HINT:

EASY EASTER STORY

Preschoolers have difficulty with abstractions such as death and resurrection. Focus on the fact that Jesus is alive. Reenact the Easter story using hand puppets. Have children retell the story. Use short prayers or simple one-line songs to help children praise God that Jesus is alive.

Kindly Capers

THEME: God wants us to be kind.
SCRIPTURES: 1 Samuel 24:11 and Luke 6:27-31

Before class, cut out a paper "robe" using newsprint or a brown paper sack. As children come to class, have them use markers or crayons to decorate the robe. After every child has helped decorate the robe, tape it to the wall with the hem at floor level.

Paraphrase the story of David and Saul from 1 Samuel 24. Then have each child sneak up as quietly as David did and cut a small piece from the bottom of the robe.

Next, trace around each child's hand on construction paper. Then have children glue their robe remnants to their hand outlines. Using an easy-to-understand translation of the Bible, read aloud 1 Samuel 24:11.

Ask:

● **Has anyone ever made you mad? Tell us about it.**

● **Did you ever want to hurt someone who hurt you?**

Say: **King Saul wanted to hurt David. King Saul was an enemy to David, but David treated King Saul kindly. Listen to what Jesus says about how he wants us to treat our enemies.**

From an easy-to-understand translation, read aloud Luke 6:27-31. Ask:

● **Why does God want us to be kind to all people?**

● **How can we be kind to people who are mean to us?**

Close in prayer, asking God for help to be kind to people when they're mean to us. Let kids take their paper hands home to remind them to be kind to others.

Get out of the storytelling rut with this idea. Have children bring sleeping bags, stuffed animals, slippers, and robes. Hang yellow poster-board stars or glow-in-the-dark stars from the ceiling. Darken the room, if possible, and use a flashlight to read a Christian book or Bible story. Connect the story to a simple Scripture.

Love Bugs

THEME: God wants us to love one another.
SCRIPTURE: John 13:34-35

Showing love to others isn't just for Valentine's Day. Jesus commands us to "love each other" every day so that "people will know that you are my followers" (John 13:34-35).

Use this devotion to help your class consider new ways to express love to others.

Prepare gelatin according to the directions on the box. For each member of the class, fill one small bowl or cup with the gelatin and chill several hours or until thoroughly set. Unmold each serving onto a plate, and have each child create a "love bug" with his or her gelatin. Provide food items such as pretzels (for legs), whipped cream (for hair), licorice whips (for mouths), and raisins (for eyes and noses).

When everyone has completed a love bug, ask:
- **What happens when real bugs bite people?**
- **What would happen if a "love bug" bit someone?**

Read aloud John 13:34-35. Then ask:
- **Why does Jesus want us to show love to each other?**
- **How can we show others we've been "bitten" by Jesus' love?**

Pull out spoons, and let kids eat their love bugs for a treat. As kids eat, have them take turns telling ways to show God's love to family members, friends, and others.

Then thank God for showing us love. Ask God to help children show they've been bitten by God's love each day of the week.

God Made Everything

THEME: God created our world.
SCRIPTURE: Genesis 1

Paraphrase Genesis 1. Tell children that God made everything out of nothing. Then take them on a walk outside to look at the things God has made. Teach the children this simple "Call and Response":

Leader: Who made this? *(Point to something such as grass, the sky, trees, or birds.)*
Children: God did!
Leader: So what do we say?
Children: What a great God!

Continue this process with several things God has made. End with a group cheer and applause for God.

The Lost Coin

THEME: God loves us all the same.
SCRIPTURE: Luke 15:8-10

Here are two ways to teach the parable of the lost coin to your preschoolers.

■ **IT'S MINE**—Before class, hide five foil-covered candy coins in the room for each child. You could also use silver juice lids as coins. After children arrive, have them each find five coins. Then have kids sit in a circle, set their coins on the floor in front of them, and close their eyes. Take one coin away from each child.

Have children open their eyes. After children realize some of their coins are missing, ask:

● **How did you feel when you saw that one of your coins was gone?**

Read aloud Luke 15:8-10. Then ask:

● **How do you think this woman felt when she lost her coin?**

● **Why was she so happy when she found her coin?**

Give children's coins back to them. Say: **Jesus is sad when one of us chooses not to stay with him and follow him. Jesus searches and searches for anyone who isn't following him. And Jesus brings that person back to follow him. You are Jesus' treasure, and Jesus will search for you if you ever decide not to follow him.**

Let children keep their coins.

■ **THE MISPLACED MONEY**—Before class, collect one light-colored children's sock for each child in your class (children's mothers may have an abundance of these). For each child, hide one foil-covered candy coin in the room.

When children arrive, give them each a sock and have them wear the socks as hand puppets. Help children decorate their socks with markers to look like women. Cut small slits on the sides of each child's sock, one for the child's thumb to poke through and the other for the pinkie finger.

Read aloud Luke 15:8-10. After the story, have children each search for one coin with their hand puppets. Once they each find one coin, have them return to the story area with their puppets holding the coins. Have kids place the coins in a designated container. Talk about how important we are to Jesus and how much Jesus wants us to love and follow him.

Encourage children to take their sock puppets and one coin each home. Tell them they can play this Hide and Seek game with their families as they tell their families the story.

Let Your Light Shine

THEME: We can stay close to God.
SCRIPTURE: Matthew 5:16

Turn on a lamp, and read the Scripture aloud. Say: **God wants each of us to be a light for him—a light that shines brightly to show the world God's love. But sometimes we sin or do bad things and our light doesn't shine. So we need help to keep our light shining.** Give every three or four children in your class a glow-in-the-dark item.

Ask:

● **How can you get these things to glow in the dark?**

After kids respond, have them hold their items close to the lamp. Then turn off the lamp and the overhead light.

Say: **In order for your things to glow, they have to be close to the light. The same is true for us as Christians. In order for us to shine, we have to be close to the light in our lives—God.** Ask:

● **How can we get close to God this week?**

Say: **Let's pray. God, help us do the things we've said today to get close to you. Help us shine with your light for the world to see. Amen.**

No Hiding Place

THEME: We can tell God everything.
SCRIPTURE: Genesis 3:1-13

You'll need a Bible and a cover such as a large tarp, sheet, or parachute.

Say: **Let's see if we can hide from God. I've brought something I think might help us do that.** Get beneath the cover with the kids. Ask:

● **Have we hidden from God?**

● **Can God see us under here? Why or why not?**

Say: **We can't hide from God; he can see us anywhere we go or anywhere we hide.** Remove the cover, and read the Scripture aloud.

Say: **When Adam and Eve disobeyed God, they tried to hide themselves from God.** Ask:

● **Have you ever done anything bad and then tried to hide?**

● **Do you think God wants us to hide from him when we do something wrong?**

Say: **God knows when we do something wrong, but he wants us to talk to him about it and not try to hide from him. God doesn't want to punish us. God wants to forgive us and help us change. When we talk to God in prayer and don't hide, God can help us grow to be stronger Christians.**

Let's pray. Thank you, God, for knowing everything about us. Help us talk to you when we do something wrong so you can forgive us. Amen.

BIBLE STORY STRETCHERS

No Lyin'

THEME: Daniel
SCRIPTURE: Daniel 6

Add spark to a lesson about Daniel with these ideas:

■**COSTUMES**—Make lion masks from paper plates. Have each child draw a lion face on a plate. Then help kids cut holes for eyes, noses, and mouths. Tie masks on with yarn. Make lion bodies from brown grocery sacks. Cut holes in the bottom and sides of the sacks as openings for heads and arms. Staple paper tails to the backs.

■**SETTING**—Make an iron grate from a large piece of gray fabric. Hang this across a room corner to "cage the lions."

■ **DECORATIONS**—Buy plastic foam balls covered with gold satin. Give each child a plastic foam ball. Have children add golden yarn "manes," plastic eyes, and noses drawn with markers. Or have children color lion faces on coffee filters, making the outer circles lions' manes. Craft angel decorations from plastic spoons with fabric gowns glued on. Hang the decorations in your room to remind your class of how God took care of Daniel.

■ **PROGRAM**—Have children wear their costumes as they reenact the Daniel story for their parents.

Ark Learning Center

THEME: Noah
SCRIPTURE: Genesis 6–9

Bring this familiar story to life for preschoolers with an ongoing learning center.

Construct a simple "ark" from a large appliance box (a refrigerator box works best). Cut off one of the long sides of the box, then place the box with the open side up. Cover the outside of the box with white or brown paper, and draw "boards" all the way around so the box looks like Noah's ark. To create the door, leave one of the ends open or fix the lid so it can be taken off.

Each week, complete one or more of the following activities in the ark learning center:

● Have children bring stuffed animals from home to fill the ark;

● Make birds from construction paper, and place them in the ark;

● Use paper plates to make several kinds of fish;

● Have children draw "friendly" snakes, spiders, and other unfavorable passengers;

● Talk about the types of food Noah and his family had to gather for all the creatures;

● Pack a sack lunch for each child with fresh water to drink. Then board the ark for the big flood;

● Tell the story of Noah and his ark from Genesis 6–9. Play a recording of a thunderstorm, flash the lights off and on, and sprinkle a few drops of water on the children; and

● Make sure to close your study of Noah with the safe landing of the ark and God's promise of faithfulness.

Follow the Leader

THEME: Real friends love each other.
SCRIPTURE: Proverbs 17:17

Read aloud the first part of Proverbs 17:17: "A friend loves you all the time." Have children think of their favorite friends and how happy their friends make them feel.

While playing a cassette of praise music, have kids form a circle and lead them in the following movements in time with the music:

- Clap your hands.
- Pat your knees.
- Tap a neighbor's shoulders.
- Tap another child's shoulders.
- Tap your own shoulders.
- Shake a neighbor's hand.
- Hold hands with a partner, and turn in a circle.
- Put your hands on both of your neighbors' shoulders.

To close, have everyone take three steps inside the circle for a giant squeeze as they say together, "Thanks for friendships."

Love That Lasts

THEME: Zacchaeus
SCRIPTURE: Luke 19:1-10

Use the following ideas to add zest to the story of Zacchaeus.

■ **SETTING**—From brown poster board, cut out a sycamore tree trunk that is three feet tall. Use a marker to draw vertical lines of "bark" on the tree trunk. Tape the trunk to the wall. Then tape inflated green balloons to the top of the tree for leaves. Sit with the children at the foot of the sycamore tree during the lesson.

■ **BIBLE ACTIVITY**—Have children sit in a circle. Tell children a paraphrase of Luke 19:1-10. Afterward, establish a rhythm by having children slap their thighs twice and clap once. Once the rhythm is comfortable, introduce this chant:

Je-sus knew Za-cchae-us,
Je-sus knows (child's name).

Name any child. Then have all the children chant the first line and the chosen child chant the second line, naming the child to his or her left. Continue this pattern until all children have been named. Finish the chant by shouting together "you and me."

■**CRAFT**—Cut a 6-inch Zacchaeus figure out of poster board for each child. Punch holes in each figure's hands and feet. Have each child decorate his or her "Zacchaeus." Then help each child thread a 3-foot length of yarn through Zacchaeus' right foot and right hand, loop the yarn over his head, and thread the yarn around through his left hand and left foot. Tie a bead to each end of the yarn. Have children take turns looping their yarn over a doorknob. As each child pulls the strings out to the sides, Zacchaeus will climb.

Might and Right

THEME: Samson
SCRIPTURE: Judges 14–16

Before a lesson about Samson from Judges 14–16, draw an outline of Samson's head and torso on a large sheet of poster board. Cut out the outline, and color Samson's facial features and clothes. Glue short strands of dark yarn on Samson's forehead for hair. Glue long strands close together on the top of Samson's head so some yarn dangles like hair. Also, cut 8-inch pieces from the legs of nylon hose. Tie a knot in one end of each hose piece.

When children arrive, give them each two hose pieces. Have them stuff the hose pieces with newspaper. Help them tie the other end of each piece. Then have each child tuck one hose piece into each of his or her shirt sleeves to make pretend muscles.

Tell the story of Samson to children. During the appropriate time, lay "Samson" on the table with his hair hanging over the edge. Quietly sneak up to Samson, and cut the long strands of yarn. Or let children quietly take turns cutting the hair.

Children love interacting with stories. Lead children in the motions of the following action stories, and watch as Bible truths and adventures come alive!

Never Needy

THEME: Abraham
SCRIPTURE: Genesis 22:1-19

Add a little adventure to your study of Abraham with these simple steps.

■**BIBLE ACTIVITY**—Before this activity, hide winter clothing items such as hats, mittens, gloves, and scarves around the room. Say: **Today, we're going to learn that God gives us what we need. Let's pretend it's very cold.** *(Take time to pretend by shivering and rubbing your hands together.)* **I've hidden things all around this room that God has given us to get warm. But you have to look for the things.**

Lead kids in hunting for the hidden items. After kids find all the clothing, have them put the clothes on. Then paraphrase the story from Genesis 22:1-19. Focus on how God gave Abraham what he needed.

■**CRAFT**—Before class, cut toilet tissue rolls into 2-inch sections. You'll need one section for each child. You'll also need one chenille wire, cut in half, for each child.

Give each child one section of the toilet tissue roll, one chenille wire cut in half, and several cotton balls. You'll also need glue sticks for children to share.

Tell children they'll be making lambs to remind them of how God gave Abraham a lamb when he needed one. Help children apply glue to their rolls. Show them how to bend and attach their chenille wires to make legs. Then have them stick on cotton balls to make soft, furry lambs. For extra fun, provide wiggly eyes for children to attach. As the children work, reinforce this idea: "God gives us what we need."

Tender Tentmakers

THEME: Priscilla and Aquila
SCRIPTURE: Acts 18

Introduce your class to Priscilla and Aquila with these fun ideas.

■**BIBLE ACTIVITY**—Set up a tent in the classroom, or hang blankets over furniture to create a tent.

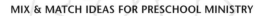

Gather everyone inside the tent. Ask:
- ● **Have you ever slept in a tent?**
  - ● **Do you know how to make a tent?**
    - ● **What would you need to make a tent?**

Say: **Long ago, a man named Paul traveled around telling everyone about Jesus. A couple Paul met, named Priscilla and Aquila, worked as tentmakers. They helped Paul by letting him stay in their home. Paul helped Priscilla and Aquila make tents. Paul, Priscilla, and Aquila showed their love for God by helping each other.** Ask:
- ● **How can you help others?**

■**CRAFT**—Give each child an 8-by-11-inch piece of poster board. Have children fold their pieces of poster board letter-style so the pieces have three sections. Have kids color their poster board. Then help the kids punch holes in both of the 8-inch edges of their pieces of poster board. Have kids "sew" these together with shoelaces.

Use a felt pen to draw faces on two of each child's fingers. These finger-people puppets can play inside the tents. Have kids use their puppets to show how to help each other.

Animal Adventures

THEME: Noah
SCRIPTURE: Genesis 6:8–9:17

Plan an all-day summer event to finish a unit about Noah. Invite children to wear their bathing suits to church on the day of your event. Then try as many of these wild, wet, and wacky ideas as you like. (Games are adapted from Group's *Fidget Busters* book.)

■**GAMES**

Into the Ark—Secretly assign pairs of children the same animal names. Kids must find their animal partners.

Rainbow Line—Give children scarves or cloth scraps of different colors. Call out the order of colors you want. Then children must line up in that order. Or have kids line up according to the dominant colors on their bathing suits as you call out colors.

Wet and Wild—Give "Noah" and his "wife" spray bottles. Other children are animals. The last two animals to be sprayed by Noah and his wife get to have the spray bottles in the next round.

Rainbow Tongues—Use presweetened powdered-drink mixes to color children's tongues. Call out colors, and have kids gather in groups according to their colors. Or call out various color arrangements, such as "purple, red, and orange," and have kids form groups with only those colors.

Frozen-Water Secret—One child is "Noah." The rest of the children form a circle and secretly pass an ice cube around. Noah tries to guess who has the cube before it melts.

Fill Noah's Ark—In this relay, teams pass ice cubes until their "arks" (buckets or large bowls) are filled.

Splish-Splash—Children fill cups with water and run around a simple obstacle course. See who has the most water in his or her cup at the end.

■SNACKS

Decorate a cake with colored candies to look like a rainbow. Or put a toy ark and animal crackers on top of a cake. Serve Raindrop Punch (lemon-lime soda with blue food coloring) and "animal foods" such as carrots, celery, and other fresh vegetables or fruits.

Happy Birthday, Jesus!

THEME: Jesus' birth
SCRIPTURE: Luke 2:1-20

Celebrate the Christmas season with these fun ideas.

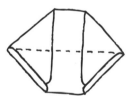

■**BIBLE ACTIVITY**—Show children an empty manger. Say: **A manger is a food dish for cows. But for baby Jesus, it was a bed. Jesus came to earth and taught us how to be kind.**

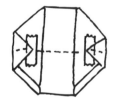

Have children take turns placing some straw in the manger as they tell about a time they were kind to someone. Afterward, place a small doll in the manger.

Paraphrase the story from Luke 2:1-20.

■**CRAFT**—Give each child an envelope with the flap cut off, some modeling dough, and a small gingerbread-man cookie cutter. Help each child cut out a modeling-dough figure. Give kids crayons to color their envelopes. Fold and tape the lower corner of each envelope so it lies flat on the side fold of the envelope. This will enable the envelope to stand up as a "manger." Give each child a shredded wheat biscuit to break up into his or her manger for straw. Have children place their figures on top of their straw.

Answered Prayers

THEME: Elijah
SCRIPTURE: 1 Kings 18

Have fun with the story of Elijah by using this "thumbs-up" story!

■ **BIBLE ACTIVITY**—Read the following story one line at a time, and pause for children to follow your thumbs-up signal or thumbs-down signal.

There was a mean king named Ahab. *(Thumbs down)* Ahab didn't believe in the real God. *(Thumbs down)* God's people listened to the mean king. *(Thumbs down)* God sent Elijah to talk to the king. *(Thumbs up)* The mean king wouldn't listen. *(Thumbs down)* There was a great contest to see which God was real. *(Thumbs up)* The god who sent fire would be the real God. *(Thumbs up)* The king's men prayed for fire. *(Thumbs down)* Nothing happened! *(Thumbs up)* Elijah prayed for fire. *(Thumbs up)* And our God sent fire! *(Thumbs up)* Elijah and the real god, our God, won the contest. *(Thumbs up)* And God's people started to listen to God again. *(Thumbs up)*

After the story, ask:
● **How do you think Elijah felt when he went to talk to the mean king?**
● **How do you think Elijah felt when God answered his prayer by sending fire?**
● **How has God answered your prayers?**
■ **CRAFT**—Give each child a sheet of white construction paper and a straw. Squeeze little pools of red, orange, and yellow food coloring onto each paper. Have children use their straws to blow the food coloring into "tongues of fire." Be sure children blow and don't suck. Remind children that God sent fire to answer Elijah's prayer.

Helpful HINT:

QUESTIONS! QUESTIONS!

Ask children these types of questions to get them thinking about a Bible story:

Discovery— These are very factual questions, such as "How many days did it rain during the great flood?"

Understanding —These questions develop higher levels of thinking. These include questions such as "Why did Peter start sinking as he walked on the water?" or

Application— These questions seek specific outcomes, such as "How can you serve your family this week?"

Way Back When

THEME: Bible marketplace
SCRIPTURE: New Testament

To help preschoolers have a better understanding of history and what it would have been like to shop during New Testament days, set up a market right in your classroom.

Here's how:

■ **ATMOSPHERE**—To create the atmosphere of a market in your classroom, tack colorful throw-blankets to the wall with pushpins. Add cutouts of paper trees and a large sun to the opposite wall. Throw an old oriental rug on the floor. Set up two tables in an L-shape against one wall to create a closed-off area with one opening. This will help keep the sellers and buyers separated. Wrap a paper tablecloth around the tables, taping the edges all around the edges of the tables.

■ **MONEY**—Preschoolers are eager to carry anything that makes noise. Use the silver tops from frozen-juice cans or foil-covered candy coins as "money." Kids will need something to carry their money in, so collect small change-purses or make drawstring bags out of fabric scraps. To make a bag, cut fabric into a circle with at least an 8-inch diameter. Cut ⅜-inch slits in from the edge of the circle at regular intervals. Fold the edge of the circle ⅜ of an inch in toward the center, and stitch around the circle ½ inch from the folded edge. Cut a small slit in the fabric along the folded edge. Insert a piece of yarn or thin rope into the slit, threading it completely around the circle and back out through the slit. Knot the ends of the yarn or rope together. Show the children how to push the fabric bag away from them while holding onto the yarn or rope to close their bags.

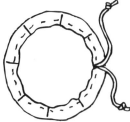

■ **MERCHANDISE**—A month in advance, put a list of items you'll need in your church bulletin. Ask for old strings of beads, belts, shawls, jewelry, or anything else you can think of to use as fun items for your market. Collect baskets of different sizes and shapes to display your goods in. A thrift store is an inexpensive place to find a large assortment of baskets. A few days before your market, send home notes asking the parents of each child to bring one food item for the market such as dried fruit, nuts, raisins, peanuts, or crackers.

■ **MARKET TIME**—Allow children to play and get to know each other as they shop in the market. Spend time talking to the children. Since preschoolers are just beginning to learn about numbers and counting, give each item the same price. Let the children take turns buying and selling the items while you supervise. Set up an area for children to eat any food they buy. This will limit the cleanup.

After you've played Market, store the items in a large box labeled "Bible Market" so you can pull it out again and again.

Drama Center

THEME: Battle of Jericho
SCRIPTURE: Joshua 2–6

When preschoolers act out stories, they become active participants and are able to remember the story longer. A drama with recycled props will reinforce Bible stories.

For the story of Joshua and the battle of Jericho, make bricks and trumpets.

To make the bricks, follow these directions. You'll need half-gallon milk cartons.

1. Open up one end of the carton. Wash out the carton, and let it dry.

2. Stuff the inside of the carton with newspaper until it's full and firm.

3. Close and tape the open end.

4. Cover the carton with brick- or stone-print self-adhesive shelf paper. (After you finish this story, you'll have a nice supply of inexpensive building blocks.)

To make trumpets, follow these directions. You'll need used plastic orange juice- or milk-jugs.

1. Wash and dry the plastic jug.

2. Cut out the wide bottom of the jug.

3. Wrap strong mailing tape around the cut edge of the jug to avoid any sharp points that may harm the children. Have the children hold the handles and blow out of the spout sides of the "trumpets" as they make horn sounds with their voices.

Reasons for Ravens

THEME: Elijah
SCRIPTURE: 1 Kings 17:2-6

Before class, cut out a large raven shape from black construction paper. Use the illustration in the margin as a guide. Secure a spring clothespin on the back of the raven behind its beak.

During class, have the children color a sheet of newsprint blue and green. This will be the brook. Tape the newsprint to the floor, and have the children sit around the "brook."

Paraphrase the story of Elijah being fed by the ravens from 1 Kings 17:2-6. As you tell the story, put small pieces of French bread into the clothespin on the raven. Have the raven swoop down over children's heads. Open the clothespin and drop bread into the children's laps. Repeat this process with small pieces of beef jerky.

Emphasize to children that God loves and cares for them just as he did for Elijah.

Stormy Seas

THEME: Trusting Jesus
SCRIPTURE: Mark 4:35-41

Read the following Bible story, and lead children in the accompanying actions.

The disciples stood on the shore of the Sea of Galilee and looked to the other side of the sea. *(Stand with your hand shielding your eyes and look far away.)*

Jesus said, "Let's go to the other side." *(Wave your arm to tell everyone to come along.)*

So they got in the boat. *(Climb into a boat, hamming it up as though the boat might tip.)*

And they rowed out to sea. *(Make rowing motions.)*

Jesus fell asleep on a nice, comfy cushion. *(Lay your head on your hands.)*

And a big, fierce wind blew against the boat. *(Wave arms like big gusts of wind, and make a "wooooo" sound.)*

25

The water washed up over the boat. The disciples tried to bail it out. *(Pretend to throw buckets of water over the sides.)*

"Somebody wake Jesus!" they yelled. *(Pretend to shake Jesus and yell, "Wake up! Wake up!")*

Jesus awoke and said to the storm, "Hush, be still." *(Hold out your hand against the wind.)*

And the wind died down. *(Let your arms wave violently like the wind and then die down.)*

And they continued to row to the other side. *(Pretend to row.)* But they were never the same after that.

Form pairs, and have partners discuss how they would've felt if they had been one of the disciples in the boat. Then ask:

● **Can you think of a time you needed Jesus' help?**
● **How did Jesus help you?**

Close by praying: **Jesus, thank you for calming the storm for the disciples. Please calm the stormy times in our lives. Amen.**

Kneel With Jesus

THEME: Knowing Jesus
SCRIPTURE: New Testament

Lead your children in this action story to help them know Jesus better.

Follow the footpath where Jesus walked. *(Walk in place.)*
Sit by the seaside where Jesus talked. *(Sit down.)*
Hold the dear children who sat on his knee. *(Pat your knees.)*
See the great miracles that came to be. *(Point to your eyes.)*
Hear glad praises the children raised. *(Cup your hand around your ear.)*
Speak with the angels who sang his praise. *(Point to your mouth.)*
Feel the sweet love Jesus freely shared. *(Cross your closed fists on your chest.)*
Kneel in the garden with Jesus in prayer. *(Place your palms together and kneel.)*

TRUE STORY
A WHOPPER OF A FISHING TALE

*So you think you've had a bad day? Read on to hear of
a ministry that may be a milestone!*

by Ann Miller

Iguess I've always felt that, sooner or later, it was going to happen: the
one colossal ministry disaster that would forever brand me as "that
crazy children's director we once had."

Maybe this was it.

I was asked to come up with an idea for an evening Sunday school
event. I prayed a dutiful—if somewhat abbreviated—prayer for God's
guidance. At that instant, a Fishers of Men Night popped into my
head. Sounds like a safe concept, right? A real fishpond in the parking
lot! Every child would catch a fish to take home and eat.

Now that's a multisensory experience! (Suffice it to say I've since
learned that instantaneous popping is not necessarily an indication
that the Holy Spirit's cooking up a good idea.)

But being a real advocate of hands-on learning, I thought this par-
ticular "inspiration" was not to be denied. Besides, it would be fun! It
would be exciting! It would be creative! What it was, was a mess!

I called trout-fishing outfits to book a date. After ten long-distance
calls, I found someone who could set up a tank for $250 and sell me
the 9- to 11-inch fish for $1.25 apiece.

"By the way," the man said, "I don't advise doing this in the summer. The water needs to be cool."

I guess since I couldn't afford his price, I thought I didn't need to
heed his advice. I chalked it up as a bad attitude.

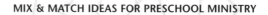

Undaunted, I found another guy who sold fish but wasn't into the tank business. His fish cost the same but were two inches longer! That gave me the incentive to find my own tank. I said I'd get back to him later. By the way, was he mumbling something about the weather in July?

I advertised our need for a free above-ground pool for three weeks with no response. It was now the end of May, and local stores were selling small pools. Why not? It was cheaper than renting, and we could sell it afterward. We got a great deal on a 12-foot pool.

Behind every intense-type children's director, you'll likely find Wonderful Spouse (very akin to a super hero), who'll spend a couple of days assembling an above-ground pool. Now, how could I have known that we'd have to haul in dirt?

Meanwhile, back at the fish farm, the trout had now grown longer, so the price was higher. Twenty dollars a pound was starting to sound like a bargain. I ordered 150 of the 14- to 16-inch trout, and my friendly fish farmer said he could lend me an aerator. He could also sell me chemicals to dechlorinate our city water.

He might've also reminded me about cold water; but at the time, I was thinking of ways to get around buying the chemicals. Someone mentioned that the ball field sprinkler system was on well water. Because of the automatic timers on the sprinklers, we'd have to fill the pool on Friday. All we needed was 100 yards of hose.

Mind you, all the usual stuff had to be taken care of during the fish negotiations. I had to write puppet scripts, hire puppet performers, publicize on the cable channel so we could reach more people, photocopy handouts, coordinate plans with the music minister, and consult sound technicians.

Finally, all that was left to do was pick up the aerator and a few blocks of ice to cool down the water that had had three days to warm up. The aerator was almost half the size of the pool. Wonderful Spouse was able to rig heavy piping to hold it up, but the piping punctured the pool lining in a few places. So we lowered our pool price by a few dollars.

Three hours to go, and the water temperature was 76 degrees—after we put in our ice! It needed to be 55 degrees. The whole community was on its way to see 150 trout floating belly-up in a leaking pool churned by a 200-horsepower aerator!

Wonderful Spouse took care of buying out the ice reserves of three supermarkets and a gas station while I got the puppet team settled in.

The fish were trucked in, but after 750 pounds of ice (that's not a misprint), the temperature had only dropped to 67 degrees.

We waited for all the people to arrive. My senior pastor said I was calm and focused when I presented the lesson. That could only have been the result of the Holy Spirit controlling all bodily functions of a person in the thralls of STSD—Simultaneous Traumatic Stress Disorder.

I'm not sure what caused my STSD. It could've been the result of 150 terminal trout, or it might've been that only ten families came out for Fishers of Men Night. I must've regained part of my faculties later, because I have a vague recollection of children complaining that the fish, also suffering from STSD, weren't biting very well.

Our youth pastor is a remarkable example of Christlike mercy. He took one look at me, removed his watch, and climbed into the fishy water which, although not cool enough for fish, was plenty refreshing for a human being. Someone handed him a net and he caught fish for the kids. Well, I suppose nets are more biblical than fishing poles anyway.

Fish were flopping everywhere. There were gleeful screams from the children and fathers. Mothers, however, expressed concerns about fish slime. Should I let them know that at the current cost per person I could've sent them all out on a Lake Michigan charter boat? Nah. I knew the fish weren't the only things flopping.

I didn't go into work on Monday.

There was someone, however, who did not stop working; who never wavered in accomplishing his purposes no matter the circumstances; who had worked through, around, and despite a frazzled children's director. Reports came in Tuesday from throughout the community and neighboring city.

Because families went home with bags of fish, they had to do something with their excess fish. People asked neighbors for advice about cleaning and preparing fish. They gave fish to unemployed friends and had neighborhood fish fries. And they all talked about Sunday school!

A couple of our families were cleaning fish in their front yard when four teenage boys came by. The teenagers asked where they'd caught the fish. One fisher replied, "In our church parking lot." Seeing the surprise on their faces, another fisher followed with, "Haven't you heard about fishers of men?" Then she was able to tell them about her faith.

God reenacted the story found in the fourth chapter of Matthew right here in Spring Lake, right before our eyes. In God's power and wisdom, he took the little we had to offer and used it to spread the gospel in ways we could never have foreseen.

When you think about it, I guess God's an advocate of hands-on learning, too!

(Ann Miller still works at her church in Michigan where they have a swimming pool for sale...cheap.)

Let's face it. Preschoolers love to play!
Play enables children to discover new
things about their world, to develop
intellect and coordination, and to try
out new roles and concepts. Use
games in your classroom to teach your
children about the joy of being in the
family of God.

Kids love creative movement. Early-
childhood specialists stress that creative movement is crucial to children's
development. Creative
movement can help
children explore ways
to worship God.

SUPER GAMES

Creative Movement

Use these tips to get kids warmed up:

★ **BODY TALK**—Play music and have children move their index fingers in sync with the tempo of the music. Repeat the process with all ten fingers, then arms, legs, and finally, the whole body. Suggest that children move their bodies in many different ways.

★ **IMAGINATION**—Play music and have kids pantomime everyday activities in time with the music. Have kids pantomime activities such as washing their hands, petting their pets, jumping rope, and getting dressed.

★ **OBJECT MOVEMENT**—Have children hold props such as streamers made of lightweight material, pieces of nylon hose, balls, balloons, or ribbons. Have children move their props in as many directions as possible, such as pretending to paint the ceiling, making shapes in the air, or writing numbers and letters in the air.

I Like Me!

Have children sit in a circle on the floor. Chant the words below. When you get to the blank, fill it in with something you like about yourself, such as the color of your hair or your ability to ride a bike. Have children join in the chant. Each time you come to the blank, have a different child fill it in with something positive about him or herself.

> I like me,
> I like me,
> I like me, because I _____.

Add hand clapping and finger snapping to keep the rhythm going.

Kid QUOTE:

When five-year-old Scott's mom read "His praise endures forever!" she asked him if he knew the meaning of "endures." "Sure I do," he said competently as he pointed to the door, "indoors and outdoors."

The "Special" Game

This game will remind you of Simon Says, but it's more special than that. The children must follow your actions, but only when you say "If you're special" (all three words) first.

Say: **If you're special—hug yourself!** Demonstrate the action by wrapping your arms around yourself.

When all the children hug themselves, you might hop on one foot and say: **You're special—hop on one foot! Oops! I left out the word "if!"**

Tell all hopping children to repeat after you: **I goofed, but I'm special anyway!**

Continue playing for several minutes.

Do You Wish?

Choose a volunteer to begin this game. Whisper in his or her ear and tell him or her to act like an elephant with a long trunk. Let the child choose the best way to act this out. Have the rest of the children guess what animal the volunteer is acting out.

Then ask:

● **Would you like to be an elephant with a long trunk?**

Have all the children pretend to be elephants with long trunks. Let the volunteer lead a procession of all the elephants around the room. Then say: **It might be fun to be an elephant with a long trunk, but God made you a person.**

Have the children respond by saying, "I'm glad I'm me!"

Continue with volunteers acting out a rabbit with big ears, a butterfly with beautiful wings, a crocodile with sharp teeth, a monkey jumping in a tree, and a squirrel with a bushy tail.

End by saying: **I'm glad you're you, too. I think God made you just right!**

Picture Sticks

Use craft sticks or tongue depressors to make picture-stick puzzles. Give each child six sticks. Have them lay their sticks flat on a

surface with the sides of the sticks touching. Gently tape the sticks together at both ends so the sticks don't slip (see illustration in the margin).

Give children felt-tip pens. Have each child draw a picture across the sticks. Make sure there is writing or drawing on each stick.

When kids are finished, have the children remove the tape from their sticks, mix up the sticks, and try to put their designs back together again. Then have each child trade sticks with a friend and try to put his or her friend's design together.

This is a great get-acquainted activity or craft.

Puzzle in a Lid

Homemade puzzles are a great idea, but the assembled pieces often separate when other pieces are added. Solve this problem by putting homemade puzzles in a lid. The lip of the lid forms a natural tray for the puzzle and keeps the pieces together.

To make a puzzle, use a lid from any container. Trace the outline of the lid onto a greeting card picture. Cut out and slightly trim the circle to fit into the inverted lid. Cut the round picture into three or four puzzle pieces.

Store lids and puzzles in resealable plastic bags when children aren't playing with them.

Rain Game

Form two lines facing each other. Have children in each line stand at arm's length from each other. Tell children they'll make rain in this game. Explain that every time a ball bounces, it equals a raindrop.

Give the first child in one of the lines a large ball that bounces easily, such as a basketball or a soccer ball. Have that child bounce the ball while walking between the lines. At the other end of the lines, have the child give the ball to the child at the end of the opposite line.

Have the child who received the ball run behind the children to the start of the line. After that child bounces the ball while

walking through the line, have him or her give the ball to the person at the end of the opposite line.

Give another ball to the child at the start of the other line. Have that child bounce the ball through the line and hand off the ball. Continue this process until half of your children each have a ball. For example, if you have eight children in the group, introduce no more than four balls.

For a variation of this game, have kids stand in a circle and bounce the balls to each other.

Wise and Foolish Maidens

Choose five "wise maidens" and a "bridegroom." Have the bridegroom crouch on the floor with his or her eyes closed. The wise maidens will form the wedding circle around the bridegroom by gathering around him or her, holding hands, and raising their arms.

The rest of the children are foolish maidens who are traveling outside the circle and looking for oil. While the arms of the wise maidens are raised, the foolish maidens may search inside the wedding circle for their oil. But they must keep moving in and out of the circle.

When the bridegroom stands, the wise maidens' arms fall and trap some lucky foolish maidens inside the circle. The rest are left out. Those trapped inside become part of the wedding circle for the next round. Continue play until there are ten maidens in the wedding circle.

Afterward, read aloud and discuss Matthew 25:1-13.

String 'Em Up

Kids will enjoy unraveling this puzzle to find a healthy treasure. You'll need a different-colored ball of yarn for each group of four. String the yarn through chairs, around and under tables, and even around doorknobs. At the end of each "yarn puzzle," place snacks such as bananas or orange slices.

Have groups play at the same time. Once groups reach the ends of their balls of yarn, they can enjoy their snacks.

Kid QUOTE:

As six-year-old Grant's pastor told the story about David and Goliath, Grant whispered to his mom, "Do we win in the last chapter?"

SUPER GAMES

Statue Toss

Before the game, cut two two-liter bottles in half. Use the top halves for the game. You'll also need a stack of newspapers. Form two teams. Have each team choose one player to be the Statue of Liberty. Give each "statue" a bottle half. Explain that statues should hold their bottles up by the necks of the bottles, so they'll have open cups. Have statues raise their bottles so they'll look like the Statue of Liberty holding her torch. Other members of each team will work together to make a pile of newspaper balls for their team.

Have members of each team stand three feet away from their statue. The goal is for each team to toss as many newspaper balls into their statue's "torch" as possible. On "go," have teams throw newspaper balls toward their statue's torch. When a ball goes into a statue's torch cup, the statue calls out "one," then dumps the ball out so more can be thrown in. The statue should continue to keep his or her team's score in this manner. Other than this movement, statues must remain stone-still (because statues are made of stone!).

Keep time for one minute and then let teams choose new statues and play more rounds.

Eye of the Needle

For this relay, you'll need two cardboard boxes, two Hula Hoops, and two small cardboard crosses. Cut a hole in each box that is large enough for a child to fit through but smaller than a Hula Hoop.

Form two teams, and have each team line up opposite its cardboard box. Give the first child in each line a Hula Hoop. Say: **This hoop represents all your toys and money. Run to your team's box and crawl through the hole to "heaven." Then run back, and give the Hula Hoop to the next person on your team.**

Begin the race. It won't take children long to see that the hoops won't fit through the hole. Let them figure this problem out on their own.

After several minutes, stop the game and have kids line up to

SUPER GAMES

start over. Give each line leader a cardboard cross instead of a Hula Hoop.

Say: **This cross stands for Jesus.**

Have kids run the relay again. This time they'll be able to get through the hole without any trouble.

After the race, ask:

● **Which item made it easier to get to heaven in our race? Explain.**

● **What did the cross stand for?**

● **Who do you think we really need to get to heaven?**

Read aloud Matthew 19:23-26, and explain how the game illustrates the verse.

Gone Fishin'

Young children will enjoy fishing for paper fish. Attach paper clips to the mouth areas of fish cut out of construction paper. Create fishing poles with dowels, strings, and magnets. While fishing with children, ask them about their real-life fishing experiences.

Jesus Loves Us, Every One

Play this game like London Bridge. Have two children hold hands and form a bridge with their arms. Have the other children line up single file and walk under the bridge. At the end of the song, the bridge comes down and catches the child who's under the bridge at the time. Then children sing that child's name. That child takes the place of one of the children forming the bridge, and play continues. Vary the speed of your song so each child is caught at least once.

As they play, lead children in singing the following song to the tune of "London Bridge":

Jesus loves us, every one
Every one, every one.
Jesus loves us, every one
Jesus loves (child's name).

SUPER GAMES

Special Rock

Preschoolers love this game. Use it any time there are minutes to fill or whenever children need to get their wiggles out. Here's how to play:

Say, **"Special rock, special rock,"** and the children become rocks by crouching down on the floor with their arms over their heads, making themselves as small as possible.

Then say, **"Become a lion."** The children pretend to be roaring lions, moving around the room.

Next say, **"Special rock, special rock."** All the children become rocks again until another animal is chosen. Do this several times. Finish the game by saying, **"Become yourself!"**

Kid QUOTE:

When three-year-old Larryn's mom told her their family wanted to go to the Holy Land but would wait until she was older, she asked, "Why? So we won't mess up his manger?"

Sticker Tag

Give each child five stickers. Tell children to play Tag by chasing other children and putting stickers on their clothing. Children cannot peel off any stickers once they've been stuck.

Play for three to five minutes. Then have children sit in a circle. If you have any children without stickers, place three stickers on their clothing. Go around the circle, and have each child peel off one sticker and tell one thing that he or she is thankful for.

Continue around the circle until all the stickers have been removed.

Head and Shoulders

Form two teams. Have teams line up for a relay race. Give the first child in each line a paper plate and an inflated balloon. Have the child put the balloon on the paper plate and carry it waiter-style with his or her arm up with the wrist cocked back. With the balloon in this position, have the child race to a finish line and back. Then have the next child do the same thing until every team member has finished the race. If anyone drops the balloon, he or she can put the balloon back on the plate and finish the course.

Blanket Volleyball

Tie a rope between two chairs, and stretch the rope across your room. Form two teams, and have teams stand on opposite sides of the rope. Give each team a small blanket or sheet. Have team members hold the edges of their team's blanket.

Throw several small foam rubber balls or inflated balloons on one team's blanket. Have those team members work together to toss the balls from their blanket over the rope to the other blanket. Encourage kids on the receiving side to use their blanket to try to catch all the balls. Then have them toss the balls back to the other side.

Continue tossing several times or until children tire of this game.

They Can't Eat Me!

Have one child (or several children if your group is large) kneel on the floor and pretend to be Daniel praying. The rest of the children are lions. Lead children in these words. Have them do the actions in parentheses.

There are many hungry lions around the den walls. *(Children "stalk" slowly around Daniel.)*

They shake their furry manes and scratch their big claws. *(Children shake their heads and then make their hands into claw shapes and scratch the floor.)*

They sniff the ground around them. They're hungry as can be. *(Children sniff the ground and rub their stomachs.)*

But the angel closed the lion's mouth. *(Children cover their mouths with their hands.)*

"They can't eat me!" *(Daniel stands and shouts this.)*

Repeat this action play until each child has had an opportunity to be Daniel or until children tire of the game.

Mystery Sock-Box

Make a durable and unique mystery box for preschoolers. Secretly fill a large, empty oatmeal box with safe, familiar objects, such as a spoon, a toy car, a crayon, a rock, and a pair of sunglasses. Leave the top off the box. Then carefully pull an old tube sock up and around the oatmeal box. The sock should fit snugly around the sides and over the top of the box.

Tell children that the box contains things God has made. Then one at a time, have children put their hands through the sock and down into the box. Have each child feel an object and try to guess what it is.

After this guessing game, talk about whether God really made each object. Help children understand that even though God may not have made the exact object, he did create the elements that form the object. For example, God didn't make a toy car, but he did make the elements for the metal, rubber, and paint on the car.

Change the objects every now and then so kids can enjoy the mystery sock-box over and over.

Circle Pull

Have children form groups of ten or more. Have children in each group sit in a circle with their feet stretched out in the center of the circle. Tie the ends of a large rope together to make a huge loop. Place the rope loop inside the circle in front of kids' feet.

Have everyone grab the rope and pull together at the same time. Kids must work together so that everyone can stand up at the same time. Try until kids can do this together.

Chair Share

You'll need one chair for every two children. Form a circle with the chairs. Have children sit on the chairs together. (They'll have to share.) Call out the following statements, and have children move appropriately. Each child must be sitting on a chair or on the lap of someone who's on a chair. After each statement, give children time to discuss their answers. Then take away a chair.

The statements are (use the items in parentheses to make more statements):

● If you have a pet (bicycle, sister, brother), move two chairs to your left.

● If you were born in the summer (winter, fall, spring), move three chairs to your right.

● If you like ice cream (pizza, spinach, hot dogs), move one chair to your right.

● If you enjoy swimming (TV, Bingo, movies), move two chairs to your left.

Hug Tag

Choose a Tagger for every ten children. Give each Tagger a hat. Tell children that the only way they can be safe from the Tagger is by hugging someone. Kids can form hugging groups of any number. On a signal, all kids must run and try to find new hugging groups. If anyone is tagged while "unhugged," that person becomes the Tagger and wears the tagging hat.

You're Special

Form pairs. Then have children do whatever you say in this action play. Pause long enough for children to complete the actions.

Look at a friend and wink your eye.
Grab your friend's hands and raise them high.
Wiggle your fingers and turn around.
Pat your friend's head and touch the ground.
Give a gentle love-tap on your friend's nose.
Close your eyes and touch your toes.
Look at your friend and say, "I love you."
Say, "Jesus thinks you're special, and I do, too."

Kid QUOTE:

Several children had correctly recited the Bible verse "He is not here; he has risen!" Then five-year-old Corey recited, "He is not here; he is in prison."

Submarine Sandwich

Get your preschoolers together for a big group hug with this game. Assign each child an ingredient in a sandwich, such as baloney, lettuce, pickles, cheese, mustard, and bread. Then build the sandwich by calling out each ingredient from the center out. As children's ingredients are called out, they'll stand in the center of the room and wrap their arms around the children whose ingredients were called out before theirs.

A fun variation is to have children choose their own ingredients such as peanut butter, pickles, and bananas. And don't forget that you can also be the baloney now and then!

Imaginary Field-Trip

Take children on a field trip—even when they can't leave the room. Use this variation of "Going on a Bear Hunt."

Pick a destination such as the beach. Ask:

● **Do you want to go to the beach?**

Let children respond. Then say: **OK, let's go!**

Have children make walking sounds by alternately patting each knee with each hand. As they "walk," call out things that they'd see on a trip to the beach. Have children repeat what you say. For example, say: **I see a swing set.** Have children repeat. Say: **Can't go over it.** Have children repeat. Say: **I guess we'll swing.** Have children make swinging motions.

Have children continue walking and doing motions for things they "see," such as riding a tricycle, digging in a sandbox, or eating an ice cream cone.

When children arrive at the beach, have them "swim." On the way back, have children do everything they did on the way to the beach—but faster.

You can also use this game to tell a Bible story such as Daniel in the lion's den.

What Is This?

Transform your preschool group into a living toy as kids imitate the Mattel See 'n Say toy.

Cut out pictures of things that make noises. Make sure that all the pictures are in the same category of things, such as animals or musical instruments. Tape each picture to a piece of poster board, and stack pictures face down like a deck of cards.

Have kids sit in a circle around the stack of pictures. Have children draw cards one at a time and give them to you.

If the card has a picture of a horse, ask:

● **What is this?**

Then have the children say together, "This is a horse. The horse says..."

The children respond with the appropriate sound for each card. Continue until everyone has drawn a card.

For a more elaborate game, cut out a large poster-board circle and tape pie-shaped pictures to it so it resembles the Mattel See 'N Say game. Cut out an arrow-shaped spinner, and secure it to the middle of the circle with a metal brad. Have each child take a turn spinning the arrow instead of drawing a card.

Worm Tour

Taking pet worms on a tour of your church building is a fun, effective way to help preschoolers feel secure and important as they familiarize themselves with your church.

Cut a variety of colors and sizes of yarn into 8- to 10-inch strands. Have each child select his or her own "pet worm" from the pieces you've cut. Have kids name their pet worms.

Have children line up, worms in hand, for a tour of the church building. Throughout the tour, explain the purpose of each room. Allow time for children to show their pet worms around and to restate your explanations to their pets.

Carrying worms on a tour minimizes wandering hands while keeping eyes free to observe. You'll find that children remember what they've learned as they gain a greater sense of belonging.

Best-Ever Crafts

More than mere time-fillers, crafts serve an important role in Christian education. Crafts

- allow children to express their God-given creativity,

- give children an opportunity to discover the world God has made,

- enhance children's ability to think and solve problems,

- build children's self-esteem,

- help children learn to listen to and follow directions,

- give children tools to apply their faith (for example, making gifts for others),

- encourage relationships as children work together on cooperative projects,

- reinforce lessons,

- remind children of what they've learned in class, and

- create fun!

Have fun with the following creative crafts as you help your preschoolers grow in their knowledge and love of God.

Modeling-Dough Table

Activities close at hand and by the door grab kids' attention immediately when they enter the classroom. Keep a modeling-dough table, including a batch of homemade modeling dough (see recipe below), cookie cutters, rolling pins, craft sticks, blunt-end scissors, feathers, twigs, dry macaroni, and other craft items near your classroom door. Watch kids' excitement grow as they experiment with different items each week.

HOMEMADE MODELING-DOUGH RECIPE

Mix:	Add:
2 cups flour	2 cups boiling water
1 cup salt	3 tablespoons vegetable oil
1 tablespoon alum	food coloring

After all ingredients are mixed, knead well for four minutes. Add a special treat by scenting the modeling dough with extracts of lemon or peppermint. Store the modeling dough in an airtight container.

Wall-Hall Prints

Preschoolers' hand prints on the wall? You betcha! This decorating idea will make a treasured area in your church.

After you've obtained permission, use a straight edge and a pencil to mark a line on a hallway wall. Then gather kids' paint shirts, acrylic paint (washes off hands with water), aluminum pie plates or other flat containers, newspaper, and damp towels.

Pour a different color of paint into each pie plate. Have children put on their paint shirts. Then show children how to gently press their hands into the pans until their palms are covered with paint. One at a time, take each child's hand and press it on or just above the pencil line on the wall. Press each finger gently so that they all "print" on the wall. You may want to let kids "autograph" their hand prints after the paint dries.

Helpful HINT:

THE CUTTING EDGE

Make cutting fun. Roll modeling dough into a snake. Have children use scissors to cut the snake into little pieces. Or have children use cookie cutters to make shapes out of modeling dough. Have them remove the cookie cutters from the dough without fully cutting out the shapes and then take the scissors and cut around the edge of the shapes made by the cookie cutters.

Magnetic Caps

Recycle plastic milk-jug caps into refrigerator magnets.

Have children apply stickers to the insides of the caps. Or cut out pictures from magazines or use real pictures of the children to fit inside the milk-jug caps. Glue a magnet to the back of each cap.

Children will enjoy taking these home and attaching them to their refrigerator doors.

Extra tip: Glue different-colored circles of construction paper to the tops of milk-jug caps to use as game-board playing pieces.

Remember Books

When your preschool class takes a field trip, has a special guest, or has any other activity that makes for a special day, extend the experience by making a "Remember Book."

Have each child draw a picture showing what he or she remembered or liked best about the experience. Write each child's narration about the picture on his or her picture. Then laminate the pictures, punch holes in them, and bind them together with yarn, free rings, or even large brads.

The books will become favorites on your bookshelf, and they'll keep experiences fresh for months. You can also use "Remember Books" as thank you cards for special guests.

Look What I Did

Place a bulletin board outside your preschool classroom. Each week, display the class theme and point to it as children enter the classroom. Once kids' crafts are finished, have kids place them on the bulletin board. Parents can help kids retrieve their creations when they pick up their children. Outline your bulletin board with photographs of children enjoying themselves in your classroom. This is an excellent way to keep the church up-to-date with the children's ministry.

Helpful HINT:

MATERIALS

Always have enough materials for visitors or someone who has trouble and needs to start over. Also make sure you have scissors that cut well. If you have a left-handed child, provide left-handed scissors.

Heart Markers

Read aloud 1 John 4:10 in an easy-to-understand translation. Give each child a 9-by-12-inch felt square. Provide scrap felt in contrasting colors, glue, pinking shears, glitter, and sequins.

Have each child trace his or her hand onto a felt square. Help children cut out the felt hands, or do it yourself. Using pinking shears, cut small hearts from contrasting colors of felt. Have children glue the hearts to their felt hands. Kids can use glitter and sequins to decorate their heart markers. Encourage children to give their heart markers to people they love.

Surprise Modeling Dough

Thrill preschoolers with modeling dough that changes colors.

Before class, use this recipe (or your own) for modeling dough.

> Mix together:
> 1 cup flour
> 1 cup water
> 2 teaspoons cream of tartar
> 1/2 cup salt
> 1 tablespoon vegetable oil

Cook the mixture, stirring constantly until the mixture pulls away from the sides of the pan. Pour the mixture onto wax paper and knead. Mold the white dough into six round, medium-sized balls. Use your finger to make a deep hole in each ball. Put a drop or two of food coloring into each hole. Gently cover the holes without squeezing the balls of dough.

Give children the dough balls. As they work the dough in their hands, the colors will appear.

Theme Collage

Tape a large sheet of newsprint to the wall at a level children can easily reach. Provide old magazines, scissors, and tape or glue. Have kids find pictures representing a weekly or monthly theme and create a collage on the newsprint.

Paper Puzzles

Place heavy paper, markers, and scissors at a table. Older preschoolers can write simple silly stories on their papers. Younger children can draw pictures of animals or places. When stories or artwork are completed, have children cut their papers into puzzles for others to complete. Store completed puzzles in resealable plastic bags to keep the pieces of each puzzle together.

Greeting Cards

Provide card stock, markers, scissors, rubber stamps, and colored ink pads. Keep a current list of people in your church who'd enjoy receiving greeting cards; for example, families with newborns, those who are sick or unable to attend church, or even visitors. (Update your list through information from your church office, pastors, or any church prayer-groups.) Regularly pass on the names and reasons these people might enjoy cards. Have kids make cheery cards of encouragement for these people. Be sure to mail these right away!

Helpful HINT:

BIBLE CONNECTION

Tie a Bible story, verse, or other lesson about God into each craft, and it'll truly help children learn and grow.

Sponge Painting

Get a handle on sponge painting. Use hot glue to attach spools to sponge shapes. The spools make easy-to-grasp handles for little fingers to hold.

Kids' Pix

Children never tire of pictures of themselves. If you've taken photos of each child's face for a room decoration or a craft, photocopy several sets of the children's pictures to use later. Here are fun ways to reuse kids' pictures.

● Cut out children's faces and place them in your curriculum's visual aids. Kids will be surprised to see their pictures again in a lesson called "God Made Me" or "I'm a Helper."

● Make trading cards. Kids can use their pictures as trading cards to remember to pray for each other. Or they can collect the cards for a "My Friends at Church" collection.

● Reinforce lessons with personalized take-home papers. Cut an oval opening in the paper to leave a space for a child's face to show through. Sandwich a photo between the oval opening and a sheet of construction paper. Glue the two sheets together. Dress up the photo to make the child look like a sheep, a shepherd, or a disciple. You can title the photo "Someone Special" or "Someone Who Loves Jesus."

Parents will love these activities because they love photos of their children—especially when they're used to personalize Bible truths.

Name Tags

Save time and money with these simple name-tag ideas:

● Use scraps of wrapping paper or the fronts of old greeting cards. Write the child's name across the picture with a bold marker, and attach the tag with masking tape.

● Write children's names on small pieces of paper. Use fun stickers to attach the pieces of paper to children's clothing. Make these ahead of time, and stick the name tags on wax paper.

Recycled Harps

After hearing the story of young David's music as he cared for his sheep, have kids make "harps" to help them sing praises to God.

Use half pint milk cartons. A teacher or older student can save these from a school-lunch program.

Helpful HINT:

THUMBS UP!

Help young children learn to handle scissors by using the thumbs-up approach. Place the scissors in the child's hand. Put the child's thumb in the hole on top and his or her pointer finger and middle finger in the bottom hole. This gives the young child more control while using the scissors.

Best-Ever Crafts

Wash the cartons, cut off the folded tops, and cover the other sides with wood-grained self-adhesive shelf paper, acrylic paint, stickers, or children's drawings of sheep on construction paper.

Slip three or four rubber bands around each carton so the rubber bands extend across the open space. (See illustration in margin.)

Children can pluck their harps as they sing praise songs.

Did You Ever See...?

Tell children the story of the blind man at Bethsaida from Mark 8:22-25. Talk about how thankful the man must've been to be able to see after Jesus healed him.

Afterward, give children paper plates and Crayola Changeables markers. (These are available anywhere markers are sold.) Have each child scribble a large blotch with a single color in the middle of his or her paper plate. Then have children take turns using a "color changer" marker to draw pictures of things they're thankful for that God made.

Have children hold up their paper plates as you lead them in singing the following song to the tune of "Have You Ever Seen a Lassie?" Repeat the song with each child's picture.

> **Have you ever seen a** *(name of picture on plate)***?** *(Children cover their eyes.)*
> **A** *(name of picture)***? A** *(name of picture)***?**
> **Have you ever seen a** *(name of picture)***?**
> **And the blind man said, "Yes!"** *(Children uncover their eyes and shout "yes!")*

After the song, make a bulletin board display with the paper plates or hang them from the ceiling with colored yarn.

Permanent Chalk-Pictures

Give each child a premoistened baby wipe and a piece of colored chalk. Have each child draw a picture on his or her wipe. Then set the pictures aside to dry.

This will be slightly more difficult than drawing on paper, but the chalk won't smear or rub off once kids are finished.

Helpful HINT:

CHALK TALK

Prevent chalk-art smears by dipping pieces of chalk into sugared water before drawing.

Picture Holders

These easy-to-make holders can be used for displaying snap-shots or little pictures drawn by your preschoolers. They make great gifts for parents—especially when photos of their children are included.

Give each child an empty plastic cassette-tape holder, small stickers, and fine-tipped permanent markers. Have children flip open the cassette holders as far as possible to see how this creates little stands (bottom-side down). Have children decorate the borders of the holders with stickers and markers. Write each child's name on the front lip of his or her holder. Have each child insert a picture to display or give to someone as a gift.

Helpful HINT:
THREADING YARN

To make yarn easier to thread through items such as macaroni and cereal, dip about one inch of the end of the yarn in white glue and let the "needle" dry.

Nature Bracelets

For a fun outdoor activity, go for a walk with a nature bracelet. Put a band of duct tape (sticky side out) around each child's wrist. As children go on their nature walk, have them each pick up leaves, sticks, or flowers and stick them to their bracelets.

When you return, have kids discuss all the treasures they've found. Talk about how our loving God made everything for our enjoyment and to meet our needs.

Ice-Cube Painting

Pour liquid tempera paint of various colors into ice-cube trays, and freeze the trays before class. Bring the frozen paint-cubes to class. Have children put on painting shirts. Then let children use the paint cubes like crayons. This is messy but fun!

Photo Bouquets

Help your children create gifts for their parents and grandparents that'll be treasured for years.

Before this activity, take six photos of each child so you can have them printed for this craft. Or have children bring in six photos of themselves that you can cut up.

Cut out flower and leaf shapes from poster board. Help children cut out their pictures and glue them to the centers of their flowers. Then use tape on the backs of the flowers and leaves to attach them to green craft sticks.

Kids can then arrange their flowers in small pots with floral foam in the bottom.

Someone Special

Preschoolers will enjoy making these special gifts for Mother's Day or any other special occasion.

You'll need small paper cups, small silk flowers, and modeling dough.

Have each child select a cup and some silk flowers. Then help them partially fill their cups with modeling dough. Afterward, help kids stick their flowers' stems into the modeling dough in their cups.

The cups become the vases for the flowers.

Fish-Net Pictures

You'll need scissors; various colors of construction paper, including blue; boxes or box lids; marbles; bowls of white tempera paint; crayons or markers; and glue.

Before class, cut blue construction paper to fit in the bottoms of the boxes or box lids. Write children's names on the backs of the paper pieces, one piece per child. Cut fish shapes out of different colors of construction paper.

Have each child put his or her paper in a box, roll a marble in a bowl of white tempera paint, and drop the marble into the box on top of the paper. Have children tilt their boxes back and forth to paint netlike designs with the marbles. Marbles may be dipped in paint several times, or more than one marble may be used to create more lines. Have children remove their papers from the boxes and let them dry.

Then have children select fish shapes. They may color and

Helpful HINT:
SAFETY

Paints, glues, and other materials should be nontoxic. Scissors should have blunt ends. Use liquid rather than powdered tempera paint.

add eyes to their fish. Then have children glue their fish on the dry "nets."

For a variation, glue the fish onto the construction paper before using the marbles to paint nets over them.

Confetti Sun-Catcher

Your preschoolers will enjoy making these special cards for special people.

Help children fold sheets of construction paper widthwise to make cards. With the cards folded, draw a heart in the center of each card and help each child cut out his or her heart shape through both thicknesses. Have each child unfold his or her card to reveal a heart-shaped "window" on each half.

With the insides of the open cards face up, have children outline each window with a line of glue and cover each window with a square of wax paper cut slightly larger than the heart opening.

Have each child cut or tear colored tissue paper into tiny chips or strips and carefully lay them on top of one of his or her windows. Do not have kids glue the tissue paper to the wax paper.

Once more, have each child carefully outline one heart with glue. Keeping the tissue chips inside the windows, help kids fold the top halves of their cards onto the glued halves and seal the two halves together.

Punch two holes in the top of each card and thread an 8-inch length of yarn through the holes. Tie knots in each end of the yarn toward the back of the card. On the front of the completed confetti sun-catchers, help children draw hearts or write messages such as "I love you!" or "Happy Mother's Day!"

Recipients can hang their cards in front of a window to catch the sunlight.

Crayon Shapes

Have children gather broken crayons and remove the paper from them. Kids may be surprised that you actually want them to tear off the paper!

As children work, place clean, used soup cans in an electric skillet filled with water. Place the crayons according to color in separate cans, and melt them.

Lightly spray candy molds with nonstick cooking spray. Pour the melted crayons into the candy molds and let them set. When the melted crayons are cool, have the children pop out the new crayons. They now have new crayons in funny shapes.

Package the crayons in resealable plastic bags.

Catch 'Em Being Good

Use this simple craft to help children learn appropriate behavior in your classroom. Give each child an empty paper-towel tube. Help children decorate their tubes with colorful self-adhesive shelf paper, markers, and stickers. Punch two holes in the top end of each tube and attach a length of yarn through the holes so each child can wear a tube around his or her neck.

Have children look through their "people watchers" to spy someone who's doing something right. For example, say, "Look at Misty. She's sharing her stickers with Jason," or "Look at Nicholas. He's listening quietly to the story."

Put away the people watchers and bring them back out each Sunday to reinforce positive behavior in your classroom.

Snow Scenes

When the weather outside is frightful, let the children finger-paint with shaving cream on the windows. It's a nice, soothing, tactile activity, and it's easy to clean up afterward. Rather than washing or wiping immediately, allow the shaving cream to dry. Wipe once with a dry cloth and then once with a wet one. The windows will sparkle, and so will your children's spirits.

Helpful HINT:
SPARKLE SHAKER

Have kids sprinkle glitter with a kitchen spice-shaker—the snap-on lids keep unused sparkles under control.

Unusual Art-Media

Make paint using God-given materials. Just mix these foods with a tiny bit of water.
- Paprika—orange-red
- Cocoa—brown
- Curry—reddish-orange
- Mustard—yellow
- Blended beets—deep pink
- Blended blackberries—purple
- Blended carrot-tops—green

Helpful HINT:

YARN DISPENSER

Use a container such as a powdered drink-mix canister with a plastic lid. Put the yarn ball inside. Punch a hole in the lid. Thread the yarn through the hole, and snap the lid on the container.

Creative Murals

Colorful murals capture kids' interest. Here's how to splash your room with vibrant images.
- Have kids help "sponge paint" the mural.
- To make awesome murals, project images onto a wall using an overhead projector, then trace and paint them.

Fun mural themes might include:
- "Faith Harbor"—Paint walls with water, pylons, crabs, and bait-shop images.
- "Spirit Train"—Have a colorful train circle the walls.

Filter Fun

For activities throughout the year, have children use medicine droppers to drip food coloring onto coffee filters. To make butterflies, have children squeeze the middles of the coffee filters with clothespins. To make flowers, have them squeeze the filter bottoms together and add stems and leaves. To make fall trees, have children drip fall colors onto the filters and add tree trunks.

Crayon Wheel

Use a Lazy Susan (usually found in the kitchen section of a store) to organize crayons.

Collect small cans, or cut cardboard juice cans in half horizontally. Paint or cover cans with construction paper in the colors of the crayons. You may also want to cover the construction paper with clear self-adhesive shelf paper to protect it.

Use a hot-glue gun to fasten the cans to the edge of the Lazy Susan. Sort crayons by color, and place them in the corresponding cans.

Set the "crayon wheel" in the center of a table, so all the children can reach it.

This also works well for felt-tip pens or colored chalk.

Don't Just Color!

To make ordinary coloring pictures come to life, have preschoolers add dimensions to each picture. Try the following:

FOR A PICTURE OF...	ATTACH...
wheels	construction paper wheels with brads in the middle so they can turn
house or church	salt, sugar, or hole punches over the roof for snow
clouds	cotton balls
trees or bushes	grass or small leaves in appropriate places or construction paper fruit cutouts
baby	small scrap of fabric for a baby blanket
sheep	cotton balls for woolly coats
sky	construction paper sun for daytime sky and stick-on stars for nighttime sky
palm leaves	fern leaves
belt, headband	string or yarn in the proper place

Best-Ever Crafts

Plastic Six-Pack Holders

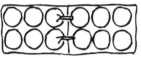

Looking for creative ways to recycle plastic six-pack holders? Try these ideas:

- **PLAY GLASSES**—To make a pair of play glasses, cut a complete holder into three sections. Then tie a cut rubber band to each side of one of the sections.

- **WREATHS**—Using yarn, tie together two complete holders. Make a tube of holders by tying each consecutive holder to the previous holders, tying each holder in the same area on the inside of the tube. After all the individual holders are connected, tie the first and last holders together to form a wreath. Paint or decorate the wreath with seasonal art. For example, you could paint it a pastel color and add Easter decorations in April, or you could paint it green and add Christmas decorations in December.

- **BUTTERFLY REFRIGERATOR MAGNETS**—Cut a complete holder into three sections. You'll need one section for each side of the butterfly. Glue one section to each side of a clothespin. Attach a fat, fuzzy chenille wire to the front of the clothespin between the sections. Add two thin chenille wires for antennae. Glue a magnet to the underside of the clothespin.

Follow the Leader

After a Bible story, put two children on opposite sides of a two-sided easel. Whisper in one child's ear a picture to paint from the Bible story, such as Jesus in a boat or Mary on a donkey. Have that child begin to paint a picture while describing what he or she is painting to the other child. For example, the child may say, "I'm painting a red curvy line at the bottom and a straight blue line at top. Now I'm painting someone in the boat. It's Jesus."

As the first child instructs, the second child follows his instructions. After the painting is finished, hang the pictures side by side on the wall, and affirm children for listening well. Then repeat the activity with two more children. This will work even better if you have more than one easel available.

Safe Art Supplies

Use these guidelines to be sure supplies are nontoxic, safe, and age appropriate.

WHAT TO USE	WHAT NOT TO USE
Water-based—, premixed, powdered, and poster paints	Oil-based paint and tempera paint can cause respiratory problems.
	Aerosol spray paint contains toxic substances.
Wet clay	Powdered clay can cause respiratory problems.
Shaving cream with children over 3.	Mentholated shaving cream has harmful fumes.
Small items such as buttons, beads, coins, and seeds with children over 3.	
Glitter with children over 4.	

SONGS & Finger Plays

Music is a wonderful teaching tool. Children love to sing and to celebrate with rhythm. Simple songs and movement can be valuable ways to impart Bible truths and stories. Don't worry if your voice isn't of opera caliber. Just tune up and join in!

Finger plays help preschool children use and gain better motor-skill control. The rhyme and memorization help their language skills. Use finger plays to help kids get rid of their wiggles, for transition from one activity to another, and for learning Bible stories and concepts.

Christ Is Risen

Sing this song to the tune of "Are You Sleeping?"

Christ is risen. Christ is risen.
Yes, he is. Yes, he is.
Risen for creation
and for every nation.
Yes, he is. Yes, he is.

Christ went to heaven. Christ went to heaven.
Yes, he did. Yes, he did.
It was so amazing;
people stood there gazing.
Yes, they did. Yes, they did.

Kid QUOTE:

When the Sunday school teacher talked about collecting an offering, she asked, "Why would we give money to Jesus?" Four-year-old David replied, "Because he paid the price for our sins."

The Neighbor Song

Sing this song to the tune of "London Bridge."

Love your neighbor as your friend, as your friend, as your friend.
Love your neighbor as your friend; love your neighbor.

(Have children hug each other while they sing.)
Give your neighbor a great big hug, great big hug, great big hug.
Give your neighbor a great big hug; hug your neighbor.

(Have children point to someone new with each "I love you.")
Tell your neighbor, "I love you," "I love you," "I love you."
Tell your neighbor, "I love you;" love your neighbor.

Noah's Ark

Form a circle, and tell kids they're going to sing about all the animals on Noah's ark. Lead kids in singing the following words to the tune of "Old MacDonald Had a Farm."

Old man Noah had an ark,
O-ee-o-ee-o!
And on this ark he had two frogs,
O-ee-o-ee-o!
With a ribbit here and a ribbit there;
Here a ribbit, there a ribbit, everywhere a ribbit, ribbit.
Old man Noah had an ark,
O-ee-o-ee-o!

Have kids act out the animals as they sing. For example, have kids hop around like frogs when they say "ribbit."

Each time kids sing the song, change the animals and noises. Imitate elephants by using arms as trunks, monkeys by scratching armpits, hissing snakes by positioning fingers as fangs, and so on.

Ring Around Friends!

Have kids hold hands and walk in a circle as they sing this song to the tune of "Ring Around the Rosie."

Holding hands with friends,
Our circle never ends.
(Child's name), (child's name),
We all love you!

Sing the song for each child in the circle. When everyone's name has been sung, have the kids "all fall down" for a big group-hug.

Preschoolers love this song, especially hearing their names sung.

The Good Samaritan

Kids will love the involving motions of this song sung to the tune of "Here We Go 'Round the Mulberry Bush."

There was a man by the side of the road (motion your arm and
     hand to the side as if showing where the man is lying),
By the side of the road, by the side of the road.

63

There was a man by the side of the road,
And he needed help. (Hold both arms out in front of you as if
    reaching out to someone.)

The priest, the Levite, or the Samaritan (point to the left, the
    front, and then the right);
The Samaritan, the Samaritan;
The priest, the Levite, or the Samaritan;
Which one helped this man? (Shrug your shoulders with elbows
    bent and palms up.)

The Good Samaritan helped this man (hold both hands over
    your heart and then extend both arms as if reaching out
    to someone),
Helped this man, helped this man.
The Good Samaritan helped this man,
And we can help too. (Point to yourself with both hands and
    then extend both arms as if reaching out to someone.)

I Will Obey

Preschoolers love to sing songs with familiar tunes. Have children hold hands in a circle and do the actions in parentheses as they sing this song to the tune of "Row, Row, Row Your Boat."

Yes, yes, yes, I will. (Walk to the right.)
Yes, I will obey. (Walk to the left.)
I will obey God's Word (walk to the middle)
Every single day! (Walk backward and hold hands up.)

These words are so simple that children will sing them to themselves at home!

Marching Into the Ark

Lead children in singing this song to the tune of "When Johnny Comes Marching Home." Continue singing this song, changing the names of the animals and the sounds they make each time.

The sheep go marching two by two, amen, amen.
The sheep go marching two by two, amen, amen.
The sheep go marching two by two;
The little one stops and "baas" at you,
And they all go marching down to the ark to be saved
from the big flood.

The cows go marching two by two, amen, amen.
The cows go marching two by two, amen, amen.
The cows go marching two by two;
The little one stops and "moos" at you,
And they all go marching down to the ark to be saved
from the big flood.

Down Goes Goliath

Lead children in singing this song to the tune of "London Bridge." Have children do the actions in parentheses.

Goliath was a giant man, giant man, giant man (walk in place with stiff legs and arms);
Goliath was a giant man. Oh, my goodness! (Cup your hands around your mouth; open your mouth wide. The last line is said with surprise.)

David had a small slingshot, small slingshot, small slingshot (pretend you're twirling a shepherd's slingshot);
David had a small slingshot. I'm not afraid! (Put your hands on your hips, and say it loud.)

David made the giant fall, giant fall, giant fall (put your arms out and pretend you're trying to keep your balance);
David made the giant fall. Down he goes! (Everyone falls down.)

We'll Be Kind to One Another

Lead children in singing this song to the tune of "She'll Be Coming 'Round the Mountain."

Kid QUOTE:

After vacation Bible school, three-year-old Faith sang, "I have the pizza pepper understanding down in my heart."

We'll be kind to one another. Yes, we will!
We'll be kind to one another. Yes, we will!
We'll be kind to one another—
To our sisters and our brothers.
We'll be kind to one another. Yes, we will!

We'll be kind to one another. Yes, we will!
We'll be kind to one another. Yes, we will!
We'll be kind to one another—
To our fathers and our mothers.
We'll be kind to one another. Yes, we will!

We'll be kind to one another. Yes, we will!
We'll be kind to one another. Yes, we will!
We'll be kind to one another–
Learn to love and help each other.
We'll be kind to one another. Yes, we will!

Paul and Silas

Lead children in playing this game, similar to London Bridge, as they sing this song. Have two people form a bridge by holding hands. Then have other children line up and walk under the bridge as the song is sung.

Paul and Silas preached the Word, preached the Word, preached
   the Word.
Paul and Silas preached the Word,
But they got thrown in jail. (Have the bridge lower and capture a child.)

Praising God will set them free, set them free, set them free.
   ("Rock" child back and forth in the lowered bridge.)
Praising God will set them free;
They got the victory! (Open bridge.)
(Repeat the first two verses several times. Then continue with the third verse. Have kids continue to walk under the bridge.)

When I'm sad (mad, glad), *I'll praise the Lord, praise the Lord,*
   praise the Lord.

When I'm sad (mad, glad), *I'll praise the Lord;*
God's Word is my sword!

Where Is Zacchaeus?

Lead children in singing the following words to the tune of "Oh Where, Oh Where Has My Little Dog Gone?"

Oh where, oh where has Zacchaeus gone? (Shrug your shoulders.)
Oh where, oh where can he be? (Look around questioningly.)
He's small like me (hold your hand level with your head),
But he wants to see. (Hold your hands over your eyebrows as if looking into the distance.)
(Stop singing and say the next line with excitement.)
Jesus knows. He's up in that tree! (Point up to an imaginary tree.)

Jericho

Lead kids in singing this song to the tune of "I've Been Working on the Railroad." Have kids do the actions in parentheses.

Chorus:
We've been marching around Jericho (march in a circle) *for the last six days.* (Hold up six fingers.)
Joshua told us to march this way, marching once a day. (Hold up one finger and keep marching.)
But today we're marching seven; seven times we'll march. (Hold up seven fingers and keep marching.)
 Then we'll all shout together (cup your hands around your mouth*) when the trumpets blow.*

When the trumpets blow (stand in place and pretend to blow a trumpet),
When the trumpets blow,
We will shout very lou-ou-ou-oud! (Cup your hands around your mouth.)
When the trumpets blow (stand in place and pretend to blow a trumpet),

67

When the trumpets blow,
We will shout very loud! (Cup your hands around your mouth.)

(Repeat chorus.)

Walls will fall down!
Walls will fall down!
Walls will fall dow-ow-ow-own! (Hold your arms straight up in
    the air and shake them.)
Walls will fall down!
Walls will fall down!
Fall down to the ground! (Fall down on your knees.)

Mary Had a Baby Boy

Lead children in singing this song to the tune of "Mary Had a
Little Lamb." Have children do the motions in parentheses as
they sing.

Mary had a baby boy, baby boy, baby boy.
Mary had a baby boy, and his name was Jesus. (Rock your arms
    as though holding a baby.)

She wrapped him up in swaddling clothes, swaddling clothes,
    swaddling clothes.
She wrapped him up in swaddling clothes, and his name was
    Jesus. (Pretend to wrap a baby in a blanket.)

The star shone over Bethlehem, Bethlehem, Bethlehem.
The star shone over Bethlehem, and his name was Jesus. (Hold
    your hands out, and open and close your fists to "shine"
    like stars.)

The shepherds ran to see him there, see him there, see him there.
The shepherds ran to see him there, and his name was Jesus. (Run
    in place.)

Wise men brought their gifts to him, gifts to him, gifts to him.
Wise men brought their gifts to him, and his name was Jesus.
    (Present pretend gifts.)

I can give my heart to him, heart to him, heart to him.
I can give my heart to him, and his name is Jesus. (Hold your
   hands over your heart.)

J-E-S-U-S

Sing this song to the tune of "Bingo."

The twelve disciples liked to help,
And they were friends of Jesus.
J-E-S-U-S, J-E-S-U-S, J-E-S-U-S
Yes, they were friends of Jesus.

I can be a helper too.
Yes, I'm a friend of Jesus.
J-E-S-U-S, J-E-S-U-S, J-E-S-U-S
Yes, I'm a friend of Jesus.

Noah-O!

Lead children in singing the following words to the tune of
"Bingo." Have them do the actions in parentheses.

There was a man who built an ark, and Noah was his name-o.
   (Make a hammering motion.)
Out of gopher wood,
Out of gopher wood,
Out of gopher wood (make a sawing motion),
Noah built the ark-o. (Make a hammering motion.)

The animals came marching up, right into the ark-o. (March in
   place.)
Two by two they came,
Two by two they came,
Two by two they went (hold up the first two fingers on each
   hand, and march one hand behind the other)
Into the ark with Noah. (Cup your hands to resemble an ark.)

Kid QUOTE:

After the pastor explained Communion to the children during children's church, he asked, "What do we celebrate when we have Communion?" Four-year-old Jason replied, "We celebrate dinner."

The sky got dark and opened up, and the rain came pouring down-o.
  (Wiggle your fingers as though the rain is falling.)
Then up came the flood,
then up came the flood,
then up came the flood (put your arms down to your sides with
    palms up; lift your hands to eye level as though the water
    is rising),
But the ark was safe and dry. (Hug yourself.)

The Commandment Song

Lead kids in singing this song to the tune of "The Farmer in the Dell." Each time you sing about a commandment number, hold up the appropriate number of fingers for that commandment.

Commandment number one, commandment number one,
There is only one God,
Commandment number one.

Commandment number two, commandment number two,
Worship no one else but God,
Commandment number two.

Commandment number three, commandment number three,
Use God's name in special ways,
Commandment number three.

Commandment number four, commandment number four,
Use Sundays to honor God,
Commandment number four.

Commandment number five, commandment number five,
Respect your mother and father,
Commandment number five.

Commandment number six, commandment number six,
Never kill anyone,
Commandment number six.

Kid QUOTE:

The children's church teacher asked, "When Jesus found out Lazarus was dead, he did the same thing we do when someone dies. What do we do?" Four-year-old Tammy replied, "We call 911."

Commandment number seven, commandment number seven,
Love the person you marry,
Commandment number seven.

Commandment number eight, commandment number eight,
Never steal anything,
Commandment number eight.

Commandment number nine, commandment number nine,
Don't tell lies at any time,
Commandment number nine.

Commandment number ten, commandment number ten,
Be content with what you have,
Commandment number ten.

Praise Him, Praise Others

Sing the old favorite "Praise Him, Praise Him, All Ye Little Children," but add verses that'll teach children to recognize the efforts of other people. Try these verses:

Praise Mom	Praise brothers
Praise Dad	Praise friends
Praise sisters	Praise teachers

After each verse, ask the children what they could praise those people for. Encourage children to think of other people they can praise and make up new verses for them.

After singing all the verses children can think of, have each child choose someone to praise this week. Then have each child decide what he or she will do to praise that person.

The Bible Is a Special Book

Sing this song to the tune of "The Muffin Man."

The Bible is a special book,

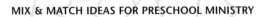

A special book, a special book.
I know just where to look
To read, "Love one another."

Sing the song again, substituting other Scripture thoughts in the last line, such as "Share with one another," "Be kind to one another," "We are helpers," and "Give thanks to God."

Christmas Carol

Sing this song to the tune of "Jingle Bells."

Quiet night, star so bright,
Stable filled with hay,
Here is baby Jesus, born on Christmas Day.
Angels sing of the king;
Shepherds bow so low.
God has sent his Son to us
Because he loves us so!

God Made You and Me

Sing this song to the tune of "Twinkle, Twinkle, Little Star."

Our God made the sunshine bright
And the moon to shine at night.
Our God made the clouds and sky,
Fish that swim, and birds that fly.
Our God made the land and sea.
And our God made you and me!

Hug a Friend

Sing this song to the tune of "Skip to My Lou," and have the children do the actions indicated in parentheses.

I clap my hands, and so do you.

I clap my hands, and so do you.
I clap my hands, and so do you.
We clap our hands together.
(Clap your hands to the beat.)

I flap my arms, and so do you.
I flap my arms, and so do you.
I flap my arms, and so do you.
We flap our arms together.
(Tuck your thumbs under your armpits, and flap your arms.)

I hug a friend, and so do you.
I hug a friend, and so do you.
I hug a friend, and so do you.
We all love each other.
(Move around the room and hug each other.)

Jesus Cares

Sing these verses to the tune of "London Bridge."

Jesus cares for you and me, you and me, you and me.
Jesus cares for you and me.
Thank you, Jesus.

Jesus wants us to obey, to obey, to obey.
Jesus wants us to obey.
I will—won't you?

I love Jesus; he's my friend; he's my friend; he's my friend.
I love Jesus; he's my friend.
I love Jesus.

Twinkle, Twinkle, Christmas Star

Sing this song to the tune of "Twinkle, Twinkle, Little Star."

Twinkle, twinkle, Christmas star
Over Bethlehem afar!

Up above the stable high,
You're the brightest in the sky.
Twinkle, twinkle, Christmas star
Over Bethlehem afar!

Twinkle, twinkle, Christmas star,
Now I know just what you are:
Light to guide us on our way
To the place where Jesus lay.
Twinkle, twinkle, Christmas star,
Now I know just what you are!

Finger Plays

Helping Hands

Recite this finger play as kids do the motions in parentheses.

I have two small hands (hold out your hands with the palms up)
And ten little fingers. (Hold up your hands and wiggle the fingers.)
God gave them to me for helping.
Wave hello to friends today (move both hands in a waving
     motion),
Hang my coat up on a hook (move both hands forward, then
     up and down),
Pick up toys to put away (reach out with one hand and then
     with the other),
Turn the pages of a book (hold your left hand with the palm
     up, and move your right hand over it from left to right),
Open my Bible to learn how much God cares (hold your palms
     up together to form a book),
Fold them together to say my prayers. (Place your hands together
     as if in prayer.)
Thank you, God, for helping hands!

After children finish the finger play, talk about how God cares
for them. And talk about how even though they're small, they
can do many things with their helping hands.

See the Baby Jesus

Have children say the phrases and do the corresponding actions with you in this fun finger play.

See the baby Jesus, born within a barn. (Bring the fingertips of both hands together to form a roof peak.)
See the baby Jesus, held in Mary's arms. (Cradle your arms.)
See the baby Jesus, star high overhead. (Extend your arms high.)
See the baby Jesus, manger for a bed. (Hold the palms of your hands together; lay your cheek on your hands.)

See the boy Jesus, little child like me. (Point to yourself.)
See the boy Jesus, fishing in the sea. (Hold your hands together, casting out a fishing line.)
See the boy Jesus; see him running there. (Hold one palm flat, and show the fingers of the other hand "running" on the palm.)
See the boy Jesus, on his knees in prayer. (Fold your hands in prayer.)

See the man Jesus, walking by the sea. (Move two fingers as if walking.)
See the man Jesus, children on his knee. (Place both hands on your knees.)
See the man Jesus, loving everyone. (Close your fists and cross them against your chest.)
See the man Jesus asking me to come. (Beckon with your right hand.)

It's Jesus

Lead your young preschoolers in this fun finger play.

Who's the baby
Sleeping soundly
In his little
Manger bed?
(Put your left thumb in the center of your open left palm for "Jesus.")

Kid QUOTE:

During our lesson about Jesus healing the lepers, I tried to explain to the children how the lepers must've felt, having sores all over their bodies.
I asked three-year-old Kyle if he had ever had chickenpox before. He replied, "No. But I've had Chicken McNuggets."

Why, it's Jesus,
Baby Jesus.
Shall we touch
His tiny head?
(Stroke your thumb with your right hand.)

Gently, gently,
Rock him gently,
As he sleeps
Upon the hay.
(Rock your hand.)

Softly, softly,
Pat him softly,
Born this happy
Christmas Day!
(Pat your finger and smile.)

God Made Me!

Children will enjoy this fun finger play.

God made the spiders (wiggle your fingers and make them crawl like spiders),
God made the trees (hold your arms up overhead, forming a big tree),
God made the elephants (hold your arms straight out from your nose with your hands clasped, like an elephant's trunk),
God made the bunnies (hold your hands up behind your head like rabbit ears),
God made the bees (hold your thumb and pointer finger together and "buzz" through the air),
God made the octopus (wiggle your arms like an octopus swimming),
and God made me. (Point to yourself.)

Come Follow Me

Have the children say the phrases and do the corresponding actions with you in this fun finger play based on Matthew 4:18-22.

Jesus walked along the shore. ("Walk" two fingers of your right hand along your left forearm.)
He watched (put your right hand on your brow to shade your eyes)
the boats at sea. (Touch the fingers of both hands together to form a triangle "boat," and rock it in the air.)
He loved (put both hands over your heart)
the busy fishermen. (Pretend to use a fishing pole.)
He called (cup your hands around your mouth),
"Come follow me!" (Beckon with your hands.)

David Meets the Giant Goliath

Lead kids in the following story based on 1 Samuel 17. Have kids do the actions in parentheses.

(Begin with your hands behind your back.)
Where is Goliath?
Here is Goliath. (Bring your left index finger from behind your back.)
Where is David?
Here is David. (Bring your right little finger from behind your back.)
Goliath is so tall. (Stretch your "Goliath" finger.)
David is so small. (Wiggle your "David" finger.)
Goliath said, "You cannot win. I am strongest, you will see." (Use a deep voice, and move Goliath while you are talking.)
David said, "I will win, for God will be with me." (Wiggle David while you are talking.)
David said a prayer (clasp your hands together)
And threw his stone into the air. (Pretend to throw a stone.)
The stone flew well (shade your eyes to watch the stone),
And the giant Goliath fell. (Topple Goliath into the palm of your right hand.)

Little David won the fight (raise your hands as in victory),
For he believed in what is right. (Place your hands in praying
    position.)

One Small Lunch

Preschoolers will enjoy learning this action story about a boy
who shared. Lead children in doing the italicized actions.

Once one wee boy showed he did care (hold your hand out to
    show the height of a small child);
He gave his lunch for all to share. (Hold out your hands.)
Five small loaves and two small fishes (hold up five left-hand
    fingers and two right-hand fingers),
"Mmm, mmm, mmm! How delicious!" (Rub your tummy.)
Then Jesus took that one small lunch (hold your hands out as
    though taking something)
And made it feed, oh, such a bunch. (Extend your arms wide.)
Lots of loaves and lots of fishes (pretend to stack food with your
    right hand),
"Mmm, mmm, mmm! How delicious!" (Rub your tummy.)

Special Seasons

Children love to celebrate! Don't let special occasions slip by unnoticed in your classroom. Use these activities to rejoice with your kids on these very special days of the year.

MARTIN LUTHER KING JR. DAY

Created by God

Use these ideas to help children look beyond outward appearances.

♥ **SIMON SAYS**—Play a version of Simon Says using physical characteristics as criteria for moving ahead. For example, you might say: "Simon says everyone with brown hair, take three steps forward" or "everyone with green eyes, take four steps forward."

Every once in a while, use a characteristic that everyone has, such as two legs or ten fingers. Move kids forward at a fairly even rate. After playing for a while, say: **Simon says everyone created by God, move all the way to me.**

Read aloud Psalm 139:13-16. Explain that we are all valuable to God. He made each one of us to be different from anybody else, and he loves us all the same.

♥ **MAN-MADE**—Help children make "stick" people out of different-colored chenille wires. When children are finished, have them link their people together, and display them over the doorway to the classroom.

Say: **Our stick people are all different. We're all different too, but we're loved just the same by God.**

♥ **A SPECIAL DAY**—Say: **Martin Luther King, Jr. was a man who loved God and understood that we're all loved just the same by God. He knew it doesn't matter to God what color eyes or skin we have. He worked hard throughout his life to make sure everyone else understood how special each of us is to God. On January 15, we'll celebrate Martin Luther King, Jr.'s birthday and say we remember and appreciate the work he did.**

Kid QUOTE:

The preschool teacher asked her class if they knew what a commandment was. Five-year-old Danny replied, "Yes. It's a G.I. Joe."

PALM SUNDAY

Paper Palm

Lead children in making this Palm Sunday craft. For each child, you'll need a 9-inch paper plate. You'll also need green crayons and scissors.

Tell children to:
- Fold their plates in half.
- Draw simple palm leaf shapes onto their plates. (Help children.)
- Cut out the palm leaf shapes. (Help children.)
- Open the palm leaves, and color them with crayons.
- Fringe the edges of the leaves with the tip of a pair of scissors.

EASTER

Resurrection Buns

Make these buns the night before Easter to serve to children on Easter morning. Children will enjoy biting into these buns to find that they're empty—just as Jesus' tomb was empty on Easter morning.

RECIPE

Soak one package of dry yeast in ½ cup lukewarm water. Mix in 2½ cups lukewarm water, ½ cup shortening, 1 tablespoon salt, 1 cup sugar, 2 eggs, and 12 cups flour. Knead the dough until smooth. Punch down the dough every hour for four hours.

Roll out lumps of the dough to form 4-inch circles. Wrap each dough circle around a marshmallow, and close it tightly. Roll the dough in melted butter and then in a sugar and cinnamon mixture. Place the rolls in well-greased pans, cover them with plastic, and let them rise all night.

Bake at 350 degrees until golden brown. The marshmallows will melt and leave a sticky syrup in the buns. This recipe makes about seven dozen buns.

Easter Surprises

Bring this basket of Easter goodies to church with you for a "sweet" object lesson that kids will love! Weave the goodies into your gospel message as you tell what each object represents.

- Easter grass—hay in the manger for baby Jesus
- Bag of gold- or silver-covered chocolate coins—betrayal of Jesus by Judas
- Chocolate rooster—Peter's three-time denial of Jesus
- Easter basket—woven together like a crown of thorns
- Hollow plastic egg that opens up—the empty tomb
- Marshmallow chicks and bunnies—new life and new birth
- Chocolate foil-covered Easter eggs—the shiny streets of gold in heaven where Jesus is

End by sharing your Easter basket goodies with children. Encourage kids to share the good news of Easter with someone they know.

Easter Drama

Have an adult dress like a character from the Easter story. For example, you could have Mary or a bystander on the street looking at Jesus carrying the cross. Have your actor or actress go to each Sunday school room and tell the Easter story from his or her viewpoint. Let kids ask questions to help them understand the story better.

Buds, Bubbles, and Butterflies

Use the following ideas to help illustrate Easter for your children. Use the following "changeables" to show how believing in Christ can change people's lives.

♥ **BUDS**—Begin your Easter preparations by bringing some forsythia branches inside. Watch the brown skins break open and the beautiful yellow flowers burst forth. If you don't have forsythia in your area, stop at a local florist and buy bulbs to force into early bloom.

💛 **BUBBLES**—Mix 1 gallon of water, 1 tablespoon corn syrup, and ¼ cup of liquid soap. Pour the mixture into 9-by-13 inch baking pans. Cut off the bottoms of plastic milk jugs. Then have your children dip the large open ends of the milk jugs into the soapy mixture and blow into the mouths of the milk jugs to send big, beautiful bubbles heavenward.

💛 **BUTTERFLIES**—Bake these to eat or use as decorations.

Combine:

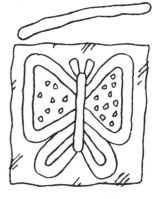

⅓ cup margarine	1 egg
⅓ cup sugar	⅔ cup honey
3 cups flour	1 teaspoon vanilla
1 teaspoon baking soda	

Put dough into the refrigerator while you crush different-colored hard candy. Roll dough into "snakes," and arrange snakes on foil to form butterflies. Carefully spoon crushed candy into spaces in the wings. Bake at 300 degrees for about eight minutes.

MOTHER'S DAY

Marvelous Moms

Invite mothers, grandmothers, and special female guests to accompany children to this party during your Sunday school or children's church hour.

Serve cupcakes and punch. To make the punch, add scoops of rainbow sherbet to raspberry juice. Then pour lemon soda over the sherbet. Have children serve their guests.

💛 **PIN THE CORSAGE ON MOM**—Tape a drawing of a woman's head and shoulders to the wall. Draw a heart below the left shoulder where a corsage would go.

Give mothers and children tissue paper and chenille wires to make into paper corsages. Here's how: Place two sheets of tissue paper together, and fold them back and forth as if making a paper fan. Grasp the papers in the middle and twist a chenille wire around both sheets. Fluff the tissue paper into a flower.

Blindfold each player in turn, spin the player around once, then have the player press his or her corsage onto the drawing where he or she thinks it should go. Tape the corsage to that place. Once everyone has played, award each mother a real corsage.

♥ **FRAGRANT FAVORS**—Two weeks before your celebration, have children make homemade soap balls. Use water to moisten soap flakes to the consistency of a very stiff dough. Divide the dough into several bowls. Add a different perfume and food coloring to each bowl for variety.

Have children shape large spoonfuls of the soap dough into balls. Place the balls on trays to harden.

In your next class, have each child wrap three soap balls in colored cellophane paper and tie the package with a pretty ribbon.

Helpful HINT:

Younger children may not know friends or relatives who've died, but they may share about a beloved pet that has died. These memories are just as important to them as memories of loved people. Treat children with respect as they share.

MEMORIAL DAY

A Joyful Noise

For each child, place paper and masking tape over one end of a toilet paper tube. Let each child drop a handful of dry rice into the open end of his or her tube. Cover the tops of the tubes with paper and tape. Have kids decorate their tubes with crayon drawings.

Say: **Memorial Day is a holiday to remember people who've died. Some people have parades to remember soldiers who died in wars. Let's have a parade now.**

Turn on a recording of marching or lively music. Have kids shake their noisemakers and march! If the weather permits, take your parade outdoors.

Then set aside the instruments and form a circle. Ask:

● **Has someone you love ever died? How did you feel?**

If no child in your group has lost a loved one, share from your own experience. Say: **When people die, we miss them. The Bible gives us a reason to not feel so sad.**

Read aloud John 3:16. Say: **If we believe in Jesus, then we'll live forever in heaven. We miss people who've died, but we can be happy if they're with Jesus.**

Special
Seasons

FATHER'S DAY

Special Dads

Use these ideas to help children celebrate their fathers.

♥ **ALL IN THE FAMILY**—Show children a picture of your family. Talk about your family, and lead children in talking about their own families.

♥ **A SPECIAL GIFT**—Lead children in doing the motions in parentheses as you tell this story from Genesis 37:1-11.

> Joseph's father Jacob loved him very much. *(Cross your arms across your chest.)* Jacob thought and thought about what gift he could give Joseph. *(Point to your head as though you're thinking.)* Jacob clipped wool from a sheep *(pretend to cut with scissors)*; dyed the wool many colors *(pretend to dip wool into several different buckets)*; wove the cloth *(pretend to push a weave forward and back)*; and sewed a coat. *(Pretend to sew.)* Jacob gave Joseph a beautiful coat. *(Pretend to put on a coat.)*

Afterward, ask:

● **Do you think Joseph liked his new coat? Why or why not?**

● **How does your father show you that he loves you?** (If you have children without fathers, ask about grandfathers or uncles.)

Have the children retell the story to each other, using the appropriate motions.

♥ **COLORFUL CARDS**—Give children white card-stock. Have each child fold his or her paper in half to make a card. Then have children tear or cut pieces of construction paper to glue to the front of their cards. Tell them they're making colorful Father's Day cards for someone they love—the same way Jacob made a colorful coat for someone he loved. Have children deliver their cards after class.

INDEPENDENCE DAY

Show Your Colors!

Set your preschoolers free with this fun Independence Day activity!

Have children don their paint shirts. Using red, white, and blue face paint, paint freedom symbols on each child's face. Use a separate paintbrush for each color. You may want to paint flags, fireworks, smiley faces, crosses, or stars.

Keep face paint away from children's eyes, and tell children to keep their hands away from their painted faces until the paint is dry.

Here's an easy, inexpensive face-paint recipe:

FACE-PAINT RECIPE
1 cup solid vegetable shortening
1 cup cornstarch
Food coloring

Mix shortening and cornstarch until there are no lumps. If mixture is too thick, add a few drops of water; if it's too thin, add ¼ teaspoon of shortening at a time.

Divide mixture into three bowls. Use food coloring to make one bowl of red paint and one bowl of blue paint. The remaining bowl is your white paint.

Paint can be refrigerated in sealed plastic containers for up to three days.

LABOR DAY

Hard Work

Use these activities to help children discover the importance of work and rest.

♥ **WORK ZONE**—Decorate your classroom door with a yellow, diamond-shaped sign that says "Work Zone." Hand each child a paintbrush. Have buckets of water ready, and say: **I have a huge** job for you. We're going to "paint" the outside walls of the church. We have five minutes to get as much done as we can—let's go!

Have kids paint the walls with water for five minutes, then gather inside.

♥ **A DAY OF REST**—Have kids pick a spot to sit down and rest. Congratulate them on their hard work. Tell them that God thinks work is a good thing.

Have children act out the jobs they do at home, such as setting the table or feeding a pet. Have others guess what the jobs are. Tell children that God thinks rest is important, too. Read aloud Genesis 2:2-3. Ask children how they and their families rest.

Say: **God wants us to rest so we can stay healthy. The Sabbath is the day God set aside for us to rest and learn more about him. We also celebrate a holiday this week called Labor Day. It's a day when workers get to rest. When we take time to rest, we have energy to enjoy all the things God has given us.**

FALL

Festival of Ideas

If you're out of ideas for fall programming, create a festival around any of these ideas:

♥ **HAY FESTIVAL**—Take kids on a good old-fashioned hayride. Bring your guitar along. Hide surprises in the hay for kids to find at the ride's end.

♥ **WIENER-ROAST DAY**—Build a big bonfire. Once things simmer down, pass out the wieners and marshmallows. Make sure you have plenty of adult supervision during this activity to keep children away from the fire.

♥ **FIELD OF DREAMS DAY**—Glean fields or orchards to gather food to give to poor people.

Kid QUOTE:

Recently, we were learning the Bible verse "This is my beloved son...". Three-year-old Alex said, "I can say it, Mrs. Jeannette. This is my baloney son."

THANKSGIVING

Many Thanks

Say: **Today we're going to celebrate Thanksgiving by cele-brating a gift that God has given us that we use every day—our bodies.**

♥ CLASS BODY—Have children work together to create a "class body." Help each child contribute one part of his or her body by tracing an outline of it and then labeling, cutting out, and attaching it to the larger body. For example, one child may trace his trunk and another child may trace her hand. Connect all the body parts until you've created an entire body. For younger preschoolers, draw and cut out "body parts" before class. Let children help you put them all together.

♥ ALL TOGETHER—Read aloud Psalm 139:14. Have each child touch his or her part on the class body and tell at least one good use for this body part. For example, a child may say, "God has given me my hand to help others" or "God gives me my ears to listen to my parents."

♥ YEA OR NAY?—Place a long strip of masking tape on the floor. The tape must be long enough so each child can stand on it with some space for jumping. Stand at one end of the tape line and have children face you. Establish the right side and the left side with the children. Then tell them you'll read some state-ments. If they answer yes, they must jump to the right of the line. If they answer no, they must jump to the left of the line.

Use statements similar to these:

● We show thanks to God for our mouths when we smile.

● We show thanks to God for our feet when we kick some-one.

● We show thanks to God for our minds when we read Bible stories.

● We show thanks to God for our mouths when we sing.

● We show thanks to God for our hands when we make a gift for someone.

♥ FOOD FOR THOUGHT—For every four children, you'll need a one-quart jar (plastic is safest) with a tight-fitting lid, 1¾ cups milk, and one small package of instant vanilla pudding. You'll also need small cups and spoons.

Reader RESPONSE:

If you don't teach your chil-dren while they're young, you may as well throw them to the lions. You can never start too soon telling your child about Jesus.

—*A reader in Florida*

Put the milk and instant pudding in the jar and close it tightly. Have children pass the jar around the circle and shake it until it becomes pudding. This usually takes about three to five minutes. Encourage students to think about how they're using their bodies to help each other. Serve the pudding in small cups.

CHRISTMAS

Deck the Halls

Use these fun ideas to "spruce up" your holiday celebrations.

● Hang a string of small white lights around your classroom doorway to welcome children. Get even more creative and write a special message or trace the outline of a star with the lights! If you don't have an electrical outlet near your door, use a string of lights with a battery pack.

● Take an instant photo of each child, or have children bring in photos you can keep. Cut each photo to fit inside a clean, round juice-can lid, and glue the photo onto the lid. Then cut a wreath-shaped base from cardboard, and glue the juice-can lid photos around the base to make a wreath of photos for your classroom door.

● Cut star shapes from silver or gold cardboard or use plain cardboard and spray-paint the stars. While the paint is wet, sprinkle glitter on the stars. If you use silver or gold cardboard, use glue to attach the glitter to the stars. Attach threads to the stars, and hang them in the hallway at different heights.

Tell the Story

Make sure your children don't forget the true "reason for the season" this Christmas. These activities will keep children involved and focused.

● Fill a jar with small candies. Pass the jar around, and have each child take a candy as he or she tells part of the Christmas story. Continue until each child takes a candy and tells part of the story.

● Retell the Christmas story by planning a "Walk to Bethlehem" for your class. Map out a walk through your church grounds or building, placing pictures along the way to help retell the story. As you walk, talk about the sounds Mary and Joseph may have heard, how tired they might've been from walking, where they might've stopped to find water for the donkey, and so on. Plan your walk so you'll reach Bethlehem when you return to your classroom.

Edible Manger Scenes

Treat kids to a multisensory experience of Christ's nativity.

You'll need graham crackers, animal crackers, Keebler's Elfwiches, shredded wheat biscuits, chocolate-candy stars, minia-ture pretzels, marshmallows, one 8-by-10-inch piece of cardboard for each child, aluminum foil, blunt knives, and "frosting glue." Make frosting glue by mixing ½ pound powdered sugar, 2 egg whites, and ¼ teaspoon cream of tartar. Beat this mixture 7 to 10 minutes. Refrigerate in a tightly covered container.

Tell kids you'll be helping them create Nativity scenes that they can eat. Help children follow these directions:

● First of all, wrap aluminum foil around the piece of card-board to use as a base.

● Use the frosting glue to create a graham cracker stable on the base. Dip the edges of the graham crackers into the frosting glue and hold the edges of two crackers together for one minute while the frosting sets. Build three walls first before adding the roof.

● Use the other foods to decorate the scene. Add all the peo-ple and animals who were there before and after Jesus was born. Crumble the shredded wheat biscuits to create hay.

● Use the frosting glue to attach a marshmallow to the center of a pretzel for an angel. Glue the angel and a chocolate star to the top of the stable.

● Keep working on the Nativity scene until you've added everything you want to add. Once you're finished, you can eat your scene or just parts of it.

Help children as needed. When children have completed their Nativity scenes, read Luke 2:1-20.

Helpful HINTS for Your CLASSROOM

What works? What doesn't? Who knows better than the teachers on the front line? Take the advice of experts from all over the country to help make your teaching experience smoother, saner, and more satisfying.

I Love You in Lots of Languages

Children are intrigued with other languages and cultures. Use these expressions of love any time to let them know they're special.

- Spanish—te amo (sounds like tay ahmo)
- French—Je t'aime (sounds like zhe tem)
- German—Ich liebe dich (sounds like ick leeba dick)
- Italian—lo tiamo (sounds like lo teeahmo)
- Pig Latin—I-ay ove-lay ou-yay

Reader RESPONSE:

Major Bible truths can be taught to children without using big, fancy words. We must start teaching children about God while they are in the cradle, even if it's just getting them familiar with the name of Jesus.
—*A reader in Florida*

Just Because

Welcome the children as they enter the room, and place a sticker on the back of each child's hand. Make sure every child receives a sticker, but don't tell the children why they received the stickers.

Later in class, ask:

- **Who got a sticker?**
- **Why do you think you received it?**

Say: **Today everybody got a sticker just because. You didn't get one because you did anything special. I wanted to give each of you a sticker because you are special. Each of you is special to me and to God.**

Spare Hugs

Before the children go home, ask them if they have any spare hugs. You just may be bombarded with bear hugs. Say: **I love you and so does Jesus.**

Take a Little Time

At least twice a year, take time to visit each child in his or her home. Bring samples of the child's work, and chat with the parents about what your class does to learn about God.

92

Have the child show you his or her room and introduce you to his or her brothers and sisters.

Be sure you mention to the parents how much you enjoy having the child in class.

The Kindness Worm

Use a sock to make a simple worm-puppet. Sew or glue on buttons and fabric scraps to decorate the worm, or color it with markers. Cut a hole in a round basket that is big enough for your forearm to fit through. Keep the worm puppet in the basket.

Tell the children that they can coax the worm out of its basket by being especially kind to others. When you notice praise-worthy behavior, get out the worm's basket. Secretly slip your hand into the sock. If you hold the basket with your other arm, it'll look like the worm is coming out of the basket. Have the worm thank the child who coaxed the worm out of its basket with his or her kind action.

The Very-Important-People Book

At the beginning of the year, take pictures of all your students. Also take candid shots showing the class singing, working on art projects, and playing games.

When the pictures are developed, mount them in a book. Use a paint pen to write "The Very-Important-People Book" on the cover. Add captions and include a list of children's names, addresses, and phone numbers. Be sure to get permission from parents before you list children's addresses and phone numbers. Some parents prefer to keep this information confidential.

Each time your class meets, send the book home with a different child. Make sure children know they're responsible to return the book the next time the class meets.

The book is a good way to help reinforce the friendships that are made in class. And when new children join the class, the book will help introduce them to the people and routines of your class.

Willy Worm

Here's a way to make children feel better when things aren't going their way.

Introduce the class to Willy Worm. Use a pen to draw two eyes and a smile on the end of your index finger. Tell the class that Willy doesn't like to see unhappy people. Whenever Willy sees children who are unhappy, he'll give them worm hugs.

When you notice a child's frustration or disappointment (maybe Josh spilled his juice or Regina can't make the scissors work), tell him or her that Willy thinks a worm hug is necessary. Hold the child's hand gently, and lightly tickle his or her palm with Willy. You're sure to be rewarded with a smile.

Encouraging Words

As children are working on projects in class, encourage them with statements such as "I like the yellow color you've chosen, Sally" or "You're using just the right amount of glue, Kyle." Find something nice to say about each child. Pat each child on his or her back, or just place your hand on his or her shoulder as you talk to the child.

When kids have finished their work, tell them how proud you are of the hard work they've done.

Animal Goodbyes

Try one of these when your children leave for the day.

◆**ELEPHANT KISSES**—Pull your shirt sleeve down so that it extends about two inches below your fingertips. "Kiss" each child with the floppy shirt-sleeve trunk.

◆**FISH FACES**—Kiss kids goodbye through a glass door or window. Show children how to make fish faces. Let your "fish" lips touch the "aquarium" glass as you say goodbye. If children give you fish kisses back, make sure you clean the glass between kisses!

◆**CREEPY-CRAWLY GOODBYES**—Lightly run your fingers along each child's inner forearm from wrist to elbow.

"Watch" What You Say

Tape-record an entire class period. Afterward, listen to the tape and compare the number of affirmations vs. the number of disapproving commands. If negative commands win out, tip the balance with more affirming statements the next time. Then tape-record yourself again.

Silly Songs

Do you know any funny songs? What about funny motions to songs? If not, learn some.

Any time you get kids flapping like ducks, waving their hands, hopping on one leg, or scratching their neighbor's back, you've got fun. The next time you sing the well-worn-out "Father Abraham," replace the old motions with these: Rub your tummy, pat your head, stomp a foot, sit down. You'll add new life to an old song!

How Children Think

Preschoolers are concrete thinkers—everything is what it is. They understand life only in literal terms and have difficulty generalizing situations outside their immediate experiences. Children find little meaning in abstract concepts such as love, God, life, sin, death, and forgiveness. Preschoolers learn from firsthand experience and personal interest.

Teach abstract concepts through active, hands-on experiences that build on concrete concepts children have already learned. For example, teach love with hugs and warmth. Ask questions to help children make mental connections. For example, ask, "How do you show love to your pet? your parent?" Show forgiveness to a repentant child with hugs and smiles. Say, "I love you. I forgive you." Use terms children can understand such as "wrong things we do" for "sin" and "letters from God" for "Bible."

Reader
RESPONSE:

Children may not be ready for the "meat" of the Scripture. But the pure Gospel message is milk. It can be delivered in language suitable for the youngest age.
—*A reader in California*

Planning Ahead

Avoid the "night before" scramble to prepare a lesson.

● After you finish teaching a lesson, take fifteen minutes (after the children leave) to preview the next week's lesson. Note the theme and supplies to gather and think about during the week. You'll avoid that last-minute hunt and preparation.

● Break the lesson down into pieces. Put your lesson beside your bed. Each night spend just ten minutes reading over a lesson section. Jot notes about supplies to gather. By Friday, you'll have the entire lesson planned and you can enjoy Saturday night.

Awesome Affirmations

Every child wants to be valued. So try these awesome affirmation ideas with your kids:

● Look children in the eye. Talk to children on their level. Get on the floor if necessary.

● Reach out and touch. Nudge an elbow. Shake hands. Give a quick hug around the shoulders.

● Call children by name. Children want to hear their names spoken with love and kindness.

● Listen to every response. When children give a questionable response, guide them toward a more appropriate answer.

● Be a learner, too. Share what you're learning with children. They'll respect you for it.

Shh

Tired of raising your voice for quiet? Instead, get children quiet without really asking.

◆ **DROP A FEATHER**—Let the children have fun dropping feathers and listening for the noise they make. Whenever the class gets noisy, all you have to do is hold up your feather to remind them to be quiet.

◆ **PLAY MUSIC**—Play a short snippet of lively music for five

seconds when you want children's attention.

◆**WHISPER**—Change your tone of voice to a loud stage whisper. Then resume speaking in your regular voice after you get children's attention.

◆**RAISE YOUR HAND**—Explain to children that when they see your hand raised, it's a cue for them to be quiet and raise their hands, too.

Clean-up Fun

When a teacher says, "Let's clean up," it can be overwhelming to preschoolers. They may not know where to begin. Make clean-up a game by directing children to specific chores. For example, say, "I spy toys with wheels that need to be put away" (or red toys or round toys or soft toys). Or make a game of counting the toys as children put them away.

Another way to have fun while cleaning the room is singing as you clean. Here's a song to sing to the tune of "Michael, Row the Boat Ashore" until the room is clean.

(Child's name), *put the blocks away.*
Thank you, (child's name).
(Child's name), *put the crayons away.*
Thank you, (child's name).

Applause, Please

Kids like to feel important. So celebrate special events in their lives such as birthdays, new brothers or sisters, moving to new addresses, or personal achievements. Have the child who is being recognized stand. Then record kids' applause as they shout affirmations such as "Good job!" "Way to go!" and "Bravo!" Give the applause cassette to the honoree to keep.

Line Control

Keeping hands under control while waiting in line is always a challenge for preschoolers. Instead of getting frustrated with pinching, poking, and wiggling fingers, try this little rhyme the next time kids line up. You'll find they memorize it and enjoy repeating it when you hold your hands up in the air to get their attention.

I have two little hands that can do amazing things! (Hold your
    hands up in the air.)
They can help my mom or dad. (Pantomime helping with
    chores such as sweeping or raking.)
They can pray to my King. (Hold your hands together as if
    praying.)
But sometimes when I'm in line, they want to get away. (Start
    moving your hands wildly.)
So I think I'll make them stick, just this way! (Pretend to brush
    palms with glue and then quickly put them at your sides.)

I REMEMBER:

"Mrs. Elsie Horstmann always read from the Bible, even though she could have just told the story to us. She also talked about how she studied the Bible to learn more about Jesus. I see her influence now as I carry my worn Bible to make home visits to children."
—Dr. Mary Manz Simon (author)

Apathy Busters

What can you do to get kids happily moving on to the next activity?

Don't tell kids what they're going to do. Make each step fun, and surprise them at every juncture. Try these ideas.

● Form a circle. Lead kids in calisthenics such as jumping jacks, toe touches, and windmills. Then have them grab hands and sit down for the Bible story.

● Need to move your class from one part of the room to the other? Have them form a line and do the bunny hop, make a train, or play Follow the Leader to get there.

● If you're assigning children to different groups, give them names of things that make noises, such as cows, pigs, and horses. Assign older kids drums, trumpets, and flutes. Or assign kids different motions such as skipping, hopping, or taking baby steps. On "go," have kids make their noises or do their actions as they gather with their groups.

Ways to Encourage Kids

Children will flock to a church where they feel loved and wanted. Use these tools to create a child-friendly environment.

◆ **BULLETIN BOARD**—Hang a board that's current, bright, and enticing in a spot where all the kids will see it. Post special activities and highlight kids' birthdays and special accomplishments.

◆ **ENCOURAGEMENT BOX**—Have church members regularly put small gifts or cards for children into a decorated box. Gifts can include bookmarks, gum, pens or pencils, or homemade cookies. Make sure children receive gifts equally.

◆ **CHILDREN'S DAY**—At least once during the year, have the children participate in the adult worship service.

◆ **GREETERS**—Designate adult greeters who'll welcome each child at the main doors of your church and in the Christian education area.

Fun Transitions

Use children's playfulness to get them from place to place. As you do, your classroom will be a more positive and smooth-running environment.

Before changing to a new activity, play a few rounds of Simon Says. Children don't get "out;" they simply get another chance. Finally, say, "Simon Says everyone have a seat at the table for story time." Then move on to the new activity.

If you have an assistant, try this variation. As children get "out" in the game, they can join the other teacher to begin a new project.

Four Practical Ways to Show Love

Here are easy ways to show you love children.

● Give children frequent opportunities to talk about themselves. Three-year-old Lindsay will keep showing you her new necklace until you finally acknowledge what's special to her. Invite kids to talk about themselves so they don't have to "act

out" to get your attention.

● Give meaningful and accurate affirmation. Affirmation is much more meaningful when it's for something the child has control over. For example, instead of praising Nicholas for how cute he is, praise him for character qualities such as patience or kindness.

● Say "Good job!" often—but only when you really mean it. If you really don't like Suzi's painting and she asks what you think, point out one thing you do like and ask her what she thinks about the painting.

● Provide opportunities for children to display their work. After an art project, have children put their creations on a bulletin board for a month. Or have an art table in your church foyer so everyone can enjoy your little Picassos' work.

Important Calling

Call your workers "children's ministers" rather than volunteers. Train them in the importance of their gift and commitment. Build a small group of strong leaders. Tell recruits about the commitment level required before they join the team.

Be Sensitive

You may have children with physical disabilities in your class. If you do, be sensitive to their feelings of not having perfect bodies. Help them focus on all the parts of their bodies—internally and externally—that work perfectly. Encourage them to thank God for these parts of their bodies.

In the Spotlight

During group time, turn off the lights and pull out a flashlight. Announce that you're going to choose a "Spotlight Person." Shine the light on a child in your group and ask that child to tell three things about him- or herself: name, family members' names, and a favorite thing to do. Have the group clap for that

child and say, "You shine for Jesus." Repeat this for each child.

Attitude Check

As a teacher, who you are is often more important than what you do.

- **Be teachable**—Learn along with your children. Keep a journal of methods that work for you. Learn from other teachers.
- **Polish your listening skills**—Know when to be all ears and when to let something go "in one ear and out the other."
- **Value parents**—Let them know about your curriculum and what you're teaching. Tell parents how much you appreciate them bringing their children to Sunday school.
- **Realize that anything you say can make a lasting impression**—Gently guide children into believing in God.
- **Be proud of being a teacher**—Know that your job of teaching children God's love and forgiveness is important.

Bubble Fun

Blowing bubbles is a great way to distract unhappy children and get them involved and interested. It's also a fun way to wind down the hour, distract an anxious child, or defuse crying.

Bubbles are inexpensive to buy. But you can also make your own bubbles using this recipe:

¼ cup liquid dish-soap
½ cup water
2 drops glycerin
1 drop of food coloring

Mix ingredients in a plastic jar. Stir to mix but don't shake. Keep the bubble solution tightly closed and stored safely away from children's reach until use.

I REMEMBER:

"As one of those kids who had the wiggles in Sunday school, I can really appreciate my Sunday school teacher, Doc Eckel. He had a big smile and gave big hugs. And he was a master of acting out stories. I couldn't help being excited about the Gospel with a teacher like him. He made it come alive."
—*Mary Rice Hopkins (children's music recording artist)*

Puppet Praise

Help your kids feel important and get them to class on time with this idea. The first two kids who come to class get to wear hand puppets and stand at the door to greet other children. The third child to arrive wears another hand puppet and leads children to their first activity.

Children's Anxieties

Provide a brightly lit, warm, welcoming atmosphere. Have children come to the same room each week. Establish permanent drop-off and pickup procedures for parents and children. Allow each child to come with one security item, such as a blanket or a stuffed animal. Keep your classroom routine simple and consistent. Vary your activities within a set schedule. Staff preschool rooms with the same teacher each week—one who sets consistent behavior limits and boundaries. Emphasize to children that God is loving and in control.

Kindercook

One enterprising church had preschoolers publish a Kindercook cookbook as a fund-raiser. They tape-recorded interviews with their young chefs. The interviewer's job was not to laugh but to take each recipe seriously.

They got recipes such as these:

THANKSGIVING DINNER
  A 20- to 30-pound turkey
  15-ounce peppers
  Couple ounces of salt
  15 ounces of pepper
  A needle
  Sauce

Get the turkey at the store. Put it in a pan. Sprinkle salt

and pepper on it. Poke holes in the turkey. Cook in oven five minutes. Eat around seven o'clock in the afternoon.

BAKED POTATOES
> 4 potatoes
> 1 slice of butter

Cook in the fireplace for fifty minutes. Put butter on the top to make them taste good.

FRIED CHICKEN
> 3 pounds of chicken
> 1 cup of skin
> 1 cup of flour and brown stuff

Take the meat and cover it with skin. Sprinkle salt and flour on top. Cook it five minutes.

The completed Kindercook cookbook was photocopied, stapled together, and covered with colored card-stock. They included original artwork by the chef-authors on both the covers and individual recipe pages.

They started their sales campaign with a church bulletin announcement, and they displayed a copy of the cookbook on a bulletin board near an entrance door. Sales of the Kindercook cookbook began quickly. Parents and grandparents were eagerly awaiting the first copies.

If you put together a Kindercook cookbook, the price of it will depend on your church community and the anticipated demand. One word of caution: Don't price this publication too low. It's a collector's jewel. This venture will give you many laughs and create a treasure to display well into the future.

Discipline Tips

Smooth out discipline problems with these tips:

◆**TEACH PROBLEM-SOLVING**—Help children create their own solutions. For example, say, "DeCille, I see you and Scott both want to use the same color of paint. How can you work this out?"

◆ **PROVIDE TIMEOUTS**—Move children away from others when they lose control and repeatedly disobey. Give children a chance to regain control of themselves. Use this time to talk with the children about what they did wrong and what they could've done instead.

◆ **HAVE CHILDREN HELP MAKE RULES**—Create the rules together with the children, and post them in your classroom at children's eye-level. Come up with hand signals together that children can use to remind one another of the rules.

Pair-Shares

Get kids involved in learning. Have kids turn to partners and respond to a question you've asked or a problem you've posed. There are no passive observers. Ask kids to share their own or their partners' responses with the class.

Kid Survey

Children's Ministry Magazine asked readers to survey kids in their programs to learn what kids think about Sunday school. The top answers are listed for each age group.

Four-year-olds like:
1. Playing outside
2. Snacks (tie)
2. Relationships (tie)
4. Coloring and painting
5. Stories

Five-year-olds like:
1. Playing
2. Coloring and drawing
3. Stories (tie)
3. Learning about God and Jesus (tie)
5. Songs and singing (tie)
5. Snacks (tie)

Tunnel to Storyland

Place a soft-sided tunnel or a large box with open ends in your classroom. Place a small slide at one end of the tunnel. When you're ready to tell a Bible story, tell children it's time to go to Storyland. To get there, children must climb up the slide, slide down it, go through the tunnel on their hands and knees, and come out the other side.

When everyone has gone through the tunnel and safely arrived in Storyland, tell them what animal they're to be during that day's story. Change the animals as you tell different Bible stories. Hear the lions roar as you tell of Daniel and his visit to the lion's den. Sheep can "baa" and bleat during stories of David, and animals of all kinds can join in the stories of Creation and Noah's ark. Have cawing ravens feed Elijah, and be careful of bucking and braying donkeys during the story of Balaam.

Clean It Up!

Tidy Sunday school rooms with these tips:

- Rub dirty stuffed toys with cornmeal and brush them off.
- Sprinkle baking soda on a damp sponge to clean off crayon marks on walls without removing paint.
- Set out a bowl of white vinegar to get rid of room odors.
- Remove jam or jelly stains by spot-cleaning with white vinegar.

Learning Centers

Learning centers are an excellent way to put preschoolers into smaller groups for more interaction and productivity. The benefits of learning centers include:

- Children have a greater chance to learn according to their learning styles. With learning centers, there's freedom for children to "graze" at the centers for as long or short of a time as they want.
- Behavioral problems diminish as peer group influence gets

smaller. Any discipline problems are dealt with more easily in a small group.

As you begin to implement learning centers, consider your needs and goals. Ask yourself:

● How many centers do I want in operation at the same time?

● What is my adult-to-child ratio? No more than six children per adult at each center is ideal.

● Can I set up centers so they're far enough apart to avoid distraction?

● What senses can I stimulate in the various centers?

Consider this sample set of learning centers for the Bible story of Daniel in the lions' den. Set up these centers:

◆STORY CENTER—Kids listen to a taped version of the story and then act out the story as the tape is replayed.

◆COOKING CENTER—Kids make lion faces with squeezable cheese tubes on round crackers and then eat their creations.

◆BLOCK CENTER—Kids build a lions' den with blocks.

◆CRAFT CENTER—Kids make lion masks.

◆MUSIC CENTER—Kids make up a song about the story to the tune of a familiar song, such as "Row, Row, Row Your Boat."

Snack Prep

If you serve a snack toward the end of your time together, set out the ingredients and have kids help prepare it. Older children can spread peanut butter on crackers. Younger kids can set out cups for juice or cut banana slices with plastic knives.

"I Can Help"

When three- through five-year-olds are combined in one class, the older kids may get bored and troublesome. To keep the older kids interested in class activities, involve them in "helper" activities. This is also a great way to affirm children for jobs well done.

Have helpers do the following:

◆BIBLE HELPER—Brings the Bible from the shelf to group time, and holds the Bible while it's read.

LIGHT HELPER—Flashes the lights at transition time to get kids' attention.

PRAYER HELPER—Leads the prayer at snack time.

SNACK HELPER—Helps serve the snack to the others.

CLEAN-UP HELPER—Is responsible for reminding kids to throw away any trash and clean up their areas.

To keep from losing track of who has had turns helping, keep a running chart of each Sunday's helpers. This alleviates hurt feelings.

Handling Anger

Expect children to occasionally lose their tempers. Tell children that you see they're angry and that it's all right to feel anger, but it's not all right to hurt someone else. Set clear limits, such as no hitting or yelling. A look or gentle touch may remind children of the rules and that they must find a peaceful resolution. Redirect children to a more acceptable activity. Avoid solving each "angry" problem.

A Place for Everyone

It's coffee time! Adults gather to chat, and children run in and out of their legs, sometimes spilling hot coffee and other times just bothering some adults. What can you do? Try these ideas.

INCLUDE KIDS—Ask children and families to serve as hosts for the fellowship time. Give children special jobs such as passing out cookies or collecting used cups.

MAKE THE AREA AND THE REFRESHMENTS KID-FRIEND-LY—Serve drinks kids like, such as juice. Place a children's table and chairs in your fellowship room so kids can sit to enjoy their treats. Encourage adults to sit with children in their special area.

MAKE IT FUN—Encourage groups to promote church activities with skits, monologues, or videos during fellowship time. Have someone tell children stories.

WELCOME KIDS—Create a Kid's Corner in an open part of the room. Place beanbag chairs, children's books, puppets, crayons, paper, and coloring books in this area.

Are You Listening?

Take control of a noisy group. In a normal voice, say, "Clap once if you can hear me." Wait ten seconds. Say quietly, "Clap twice if you can hear me." Wait three seconds. Whisper, "Clap three times if you can hear me."

How Children Solve Problems

Preschoolers are still highly multisensory. They learn and solve problems when they touch and do. Three-year-olds may not be as assertive as two-year-olds; they may whine and try to manipulate adults to solve problems for them. But four-year-olds may be aggressive as they try out new problem-solving skills. Five-year-olds are eager to please adults and will often solve problems to satisfy them.

Help children solve problems in age-appropriate ways. For example, when children whine, give them choices to solve the problem. For example, say, "You may use your regular voice or you may be quiet" instead of "Don't whine!" When four-year-olds go out of bounds, define appropriate solutions. Praise five-year-olds' problem-solving skills.

When Kids Doubt

Three-year-olds may ask, "Who made the world?" The answer "God did" will satisfy them. Older preschool children begin to doubt and ask "Why?" and "How?"

Recognize that children have doubts. Answer their questions simply. Use words that mean exactly what they say. When you tell stories about Jesus' miracles, emphasize how Jesus helped others out of love and concern. Also emphasize that he is God and he alone can do these miraculous deeds. Never ridicule or shame a child for questioning. Be a good listener, using reflective listening. Affirm children's feelings with phrases such as "You seem afraid" or "You look as if you have a question."

Where's My Other Boot?

Avoid boot and glove mix-ups in your classroom this winter. Use clothespins to clip boots or gloves together.

Attention Spans

Preschoolers have short attention spans. Keep activities short— no more than four or five minutes. Provide multiple activities to involve kids' different senses. Let children choose from activities when they arrive. Use visual aids to enhance stories. Have children identify objects they see. Encourage children to talk about their experiences and feelings that relate to the story. Have an adult helper give inattentive children individual attention.

Song Dial

Since preschool children can't read, use a song dial that lets children pick out favorite songs they already know. Draw twelve musical notes around the edges of a sheet of poster board. Then draw or attach a picture in each note to represent a different song. For example, for "Joshua Fought the Battle of Jericho," draw a horn and ancient city walls. And for "Jesus Loves Me," attach a picture of Jesus with a red heart drawn on his chest.

Then use a paper fastener or brad to attach a large arrow to the center of the dial. When it's time to sing, children take turns pointing the arrow to a chosen song.

Index

FINGER PLAYS

SONGS

CHRISTMAS

EASTER

FALL

FATHER'S DAY

INDEPENDENCE DAY

LABOR DAY

MARTIN LUTHER KING JR. DAY

MEMORIAL DAY

MOTHER'S DAY

PALM SUNDAY

THANKSGIVING